# THE RHYTHM BOOK

## The Complete Guide to Pop Rhythm, Percussion, and the New Generation of Electronic Drums

by Steve Savage

*Edited by Sally Englefried*

6400 Hollis Street
Emeryville, CA 94608

©2000 Intertec Publishing Corporation

Library of Congress Catalog Card Number: 99-62-487

Cover Design: Linda Gough
Book Design and Layout: Linda Gough
Production Staff: Mike Lawson, publisher; Sally Englefried, editor

6400 Hollis Street, Suite 12
Emeryville, CA 94608
510-653-3307

Also from EMBooks:
*The Independent Working Musician*
*Making the Ultimate Demo*
*Tech Terms: A Practical Dictionary for Audio and Music Production*
*Making Music with Your Computer*
*Anatomy of a Home Studio*
*The EM Guide to the Roland VS-880*

**Also from MixBooks**
*The AudioPro Home Recording Course, Volumes I, II and III*
*I Hate the Man Who Runs this Bar!*
*How to Make Money Scoring Soundtracks and Jingles*
*The Art of Mixing: A Visual Guide to Recording, Engineering, and Production*
*500 Songwriting Ideas (For Brave and Passionate People)*
*Music Publishing: The Real Road to Music Business Success, Rev. and Exp. 4th Ed.*
*How to Run a Recording Session*
*Mix Reference Disc, Deluxe Ed.*
*The Songwriters Guide to Collaboration, Rev. and Exp. 2nd Ed.*
*Critical Listening and Auditory Perception*
*Keyfax Omnibus Edition*
*Modular Digital Multitracks: The Power User's Guide*
*The Dictionary of Music Business Terms*
*Professional Microphone Techniques*
*Concert Sound*
*Sound for Picture*
*Music Producers*
*Live Sound Reinforcement*

MixBooks is a property of Intertec Publishing Corporation
Printed in Auburn Hills, MI
ISBN 0-87288-729-4

Dedication

For Andi

# *Acknowledgments*

Thanks to my publisher Mike Lawson, my designer Linda Gough, my copy editor Sally Engelfried and my music type-setter Evan Conlee for making this book a reality. Thanks to Tad Lathrop for editing assistance to William F. Ludwig Jr., for the history of the drum set to Lynn Chu, for the initial impetus to Blue Bear School of American Music for a home as a drum teacher in years past and to my brother Marc for support both technical and moral. Thanks for demo support with all of the new technology to Jerry Basserman, Christine Berkley, Robert Blewett, Richard Bock, Martin Cohen, Steve Fisher, Liana Jones, Jack Knight, Joe Spiegel, Marcia Stevenson, Marcia Vdovin and Shelly Williams.

# About the Author

Steve Savage is an independent producer/engineer in San Francisco. He is most fortunate to work with great musicians and singers on great recording projects. In his free time he bets the ponies with the love of his life—Darlene Jody.

# Contents

# PART ONE

# RHYTHM BASICS

# CHAPTER 1

# Rhythm, Pulse, and Nature

Without a doubt, the broad appeal of popular music has always been due in good part to its outgoing sense of rhythm...

hythm is all around us. It is a part of our essential nature and is basic to the world we live in. It permeates the natural environment, marks off the passage of time, and is present in the movement of things, man-made and otherwise. Rhythm runs deep.

But it is in popular music that rhythm is most obviously and undeniably present. There it provides a true driving force. At the core of every pop song is an underlying beat or groove that instantly defines the feel of the music and tells the listener how to respond, whether to move in time with an uptempo dance rhythm or to slow down in preparation for a smooth, flowing ballad. It's the beat of the music, when played with precision and skill, that first grabs and holds our attention.

The human affinity for rhythm is undeniable. Whatever the beat, whatever the musical style, it's the rhythmic thrust that ultimately drives the song home. Think of the sound of a high-tech urban dance tune rolling out of twin speakers on a wave of funky hits, rimshots and backbeats built from loops and samples. Or the sound of jazz, radiating swing-based triplets, finger snaps, kick drum accents, and walking bass lines. Or crunchy rock and roll, with its powerful backbeat and propulsive forward motion. They all tie into an unspoken human feeling, matching the tempo and thrust of our own internal rhythms.

Take a look at the underlying rhythms of hit songs and you'll find much of what put the "popular" in pop music. When the Beatles first arrived on the scene (with a name that matched the momentum of their music) they were hailed for bringing a "big beat" approach to the otherwise tame sound of hit radio. Their knack for locking into a catchy backbeat rhythm went a long way toward fueling the fires of mid-sixties Beatlemania. And Elvis Presley, only a few years before, worked similar magic with his own brand of gyrating rock and roll (a term not without rhythmic reference), basing his chart-topping sound on a loose blend of country music and hip-shaking rhythm and blues. Or Madonna, whose evolution from disco through hip-hop to electronica has always featured dynamic rhythm tracks that have been as at home in the dance halls as they have on the radio. Without a doubt, the broad appeal of popular music has always been due in good part to its outgoing sense of rhythm, connecting with this fundamental facet of human nature.

## BECOMING A RHYTHMIST.

What this means for the rhythm-making musician of today is that a solid sense of rhythm—and how it works in various styles of music—is absolutely essential for getting a message across to audiences. Whatever your musical background, whether it is as a drummer, a guitarist, a songwriter, an arranger, or a user of home recording equipment, chances are your ultimate goal is to write, play, or record the best music possible, with rhythms that really complement your musical vision. To do this, you're going to have to learn more—much more—about all aspects of your craft, building up a firm foundation of knowledge and skill to develop effective rhythms and to function smoothly in the creative, professional world of music.

If you're a drummer, you probably have a particular brand of music that you think of as your specialty. You may have delved deeply into jazz, following in the footsteps of Elvin Jones, Buddy Rich, or Max Roach. Or you might have focused on hard rock and heavy metal, developing a shotgun snare sound and a double-barreled kick drum technique. But there's much more out there. Keep in mind that branching out and picking up ideas from all areas of music is only going to add to your rhythm arsenal, giving you the tools to work in a number of contexts and providing new fuel for the development of your own favorite drum style. It's also important to get on top of the new technology that's become a central part of many musical styles, especially the drum machines and samplers that are so often being used to supplement real drum sounds and performances.

If you're a guitarist or other nondrumming instrumentalist, you may have wandered into the world of sequenced drum parts as a way to enrich your home practicing or to add a professional sound to your demo tapes. Naturally, you're going to have to look into the techniques and beats that drummers and programmers actually use in the style of music you're

...you'll need to
begin thinking like a
drummer, learning
about the subtleties
of contemporary drum
part construction.

playing or recording. More generally, you'll need to begin thinking like a drummer, learning about the subtleties of contemporary drum part construction.

If you're a songwriter and like many others, you like to vary your repertoire and work in different grooves from song to song. Without a broad background of rhythmic knowledge, you might miss out on some exciting approaches that could inspire a Top 10 hit or at least point you in a new direction. If you happen to be stuck in a particular genre, like straight-ahead rock and roll, trying out ideas from other rhythmic formats will usually break the stalemate and get some fresh creative juices flowing.

If you're a home recording enthusiast, you've probably assembled (or are beginning to assemble) a collection of impressive toys like a digital 8-track, a sampler, and a personal computer capable of a wide range of musical construction and manipulation. When you recover from the spending binge, you'll find that all the technology in the world won't guarantee a demo tape that contains thoughtful, inspired, or even coherent music. The current myth is that anyone with a little cash can purchase state-of-the-art software, synths, and tape decks and then go on to compete in the real world of professional music composer/producers. The not-so-secret truth is that not one money-making producer today is doing it on equipment alone. If you own a tape recorder or a computer and plan on using it to nail down some effective music tracks, you may as well do it right and learn as much as possible about the drum beats, the stylistic influences, the array of percussion sounds, and the full range of electronic gear and computer software that will ultimately be at your disposal.

Rhythm has had a profound influence on the direction and accessibility of contemporary music. To gain a fuller sense of that importance and to begin plugging into the mechanisms that make rhythm tick, it's worth starting with the basics and looking at the depth of rhythm's roots in nature itself. It is there that the essence of rhythm ebbs and flows, awaiting the force of logic to lend it shape and structure. How does rhythm connect with the natural world and with our own physical processes? And how does that reflect back and have an impact on the effectiveness of rhythms we play?

## DEFINING RHYTHM.

We experience rhythm on a subconscious, purely physical level in the beating of our heart and in the filling of our lungs. We express rhythm in our walk, our talk, and our everyday actions. We hear rhythm in nature—in the falling rain, the rustling wind, and the rushing of water. We follow rhythm in poetry, plays, movies, and novels. We see rhythm in painting, sculpture, architecture, and everyday objects. We use rhythm as the essential underpinning of music, especially of the pop music that most of us have grown up with. But how does it all work? And what is rhythm, anyway?

> By manipulating units of rhythm in a musical context, we can play upon a listener's physical senses as well as their emotional responses.

The word *rhythm* is derived from the Greek rhythmos which means "measured motion" or put more broadly, "to flow." Rhythm flows as a river flows—not always at the same rate of speed or in the same direction, but always with motion. The flow of our lives might easily be expressed in terms of rhythm.

Broadly speaking, rhythm is tied into our general concept of time. Both time and rhythm share an element of movement, of forward motion. The mind is constantly attempting to place order on the passage or movement of time, and it does so in a number of common, everyday ways: we "set the pace" of our walk down the street; we schedule our activities to get them done in time. Almost any human activity can be said to have a rhythm that helps us sense the passage of time.

But rhythm can go beyond the simple ordering or measuring of time. By manipulating units of rhythm in a musical context, we can play upon a listener's physical senses as well as their emotional responses.

## RHYTHM IN MUSIC.

Music itself is a composition in time. Rhythm is essential to music—it is its basic organization of time. It is also an aspect of music that helps us transcend our normal experience of time. In a musical context, rhythm may be both the measurement of musical structure and the basis for musical magic.

The most basic elements of musical experience—such as feelings of excitement or of being soothed—grow out of varied approaches to rhythm. The linkage of rhythm to feeling is suggested in the term "organic rhythm," drawn from the vocabulary of poetry that describes a rhythmic flow of words

...in all cases, musical rhythm is closely tied to human feeling, and to understand this link we need to examine more closely the structure of musical rhythm.

designed to match the feeling to be conveyed. In music, tempos and rhythms express feelings in the simple ways that they mimic human experience. A normal musical tempo may be sixty or eighty beats per minute (BPM), the average heartbeat is seventy-two BPM, and the natural walking pace seventy-six to eighty steps per minute. Obviously, the pace of a person running will create many more steps per minute and a considerably faster heartbeat. Similarly certain kinds of music and musical passages employ somewhat faster or slower tempos. Faster tempos—such as those found in current rock styles such as speed metal and punk—often generate an intense degree of excitement. A slow blues will bring out a sense of spaciousness, perhaps suggesting the pain of longing or a feeling of melancholy. The undulating, intertwining rhythms of hip-hop may produce an edgy or jumpy feeling. Sometimes a particularly complex rhythm will suggest feelings and responses too difficult to categorize or define. In fact, a single piece of music may elicit different reactions from different people. Yet in all cases, musical rhythm is closely tied to human feeling, and to understand this link we need to examine more closely the structure of musical rhythm.

Music generally consists of rhythm, melody, and harmony. Among these elements, rhythm is the most fundamental. Melody and harmony must have a rhythmic context. They require rhythm to place them in time, though they also influence and create rhythm as part of their process of movement. Rhythm, on the other hand, may stand alone as the sole musical element, as in a drum or percussion solo.

Rhythm in music is generally formed relative to an underlying pulse (beat) at a given rate (tempo), in regularly numbered (metric) groups. This means that there is a basic unit of time organized into regular and repeating patterns. Endless patterns may be formed, within a metric context, from notes made up of larger and smaller fractional values of the beat.

The best way to approach some of rhythm's more complex patterns, especially the ones used in pop music, is to first look at one of rhythm's most basic elements and one of its most obvious connections to nature: the pulse.

The basic unit into which we divide musical time is called a pulse beat or just a beat. A regular succession of beats creates a pulse. While listening to most music we are instinctively aware of a periodic succession of beats, a *pulse*, which is underlying the musical rhythm. Sometimes the pulse is hard to hear, and in some forms of music (generally termed *free rhythm*) it doesn't exist. In most music, however, there is a guiding pulse that is possible for us to follow. The musical pulse is most often the foundation of the musical rhythm, and it comes from some very essential and natural elements of life.

The musical pulse has many counterparts in nature. On the most fundamental level, musical pulses tend to correspond to such basic phenomena as the heartbeat and walking, as described earlier. On a higher level, musical pulse can be defined in terms of dance. The proper beat, meaning the rate of pulse that we identify as the beat, is the rate comfortable for dancing (or marching, another aspect of human movement often associated with drums and percussion). Perception of the beat may vary from person to person, but in most instances any person will respond physically to the same level of pulse in a given piece of music. This pulse is called the beat.

## ACCENTING THE PULSE.

A simple pulse, however, is still lacking one of the other basic elements of rhythm: accent. When presented with an unaccented pulse, people tend to instinctively divide the pulse into groups of two or three by imagining a stress on the first of every two or three beats. The mind imposes a regular succession of strong and weak beats on an otherwise unaccented pulse. This instinct for stress accenting is closely associated with actions of the body—the natural rhythm of movement in dance on the one hand, and the rhythms of work-oriented movements such as swinging an ax or rocking a cradle on the other. The pleasing regularity of the rhythm of poetry is part of this same instinct to group into patterns or measures of time.

Musical rhythm reflects this natural tendency to perceive groups of beats in its use of accentuation, forming a simple pulse with accents. By accenting or stressing notes at regular intervals, we create units of time (time-measures), which are fundamental building blocks of rhythm. In the example below, the circles represent pulses. By accenting (darkening) certain pulses we create groupings (or time-measures) of three:

Musicians often express a relationship to the pulse in the way they move their bodies while performing, or in the way the "groove to the beat." Watch almost any professional musician in any style of music (or think about your own playing habits), and you will see them keeping a pulse—the beat—with some part of their body. It may be expressed in just a tapping of the foot, with a large whole-body movement, or a slight nodding of the head—in some way, they are translating the beat into a physical movement. And within that motion they are also probably acknowledging the subtle accents that recur in the pulse. Accenting a pulse is the simplest way rhythm reflects the natural flow of human movement. Without accents, a pulse just becomes a mechanical reminder of the passage of time.

## PULSE GAMES

The following games may help you begin to feel and internalize the relationship of accents to pulse in the same way that a drummer might. (They will also prepare you for the following chapters on notation and basic rhythms). By using circles to indicate pulse beats and darker and lighter shadings to indicate accentuation, you can begin to perform some basic accented pulses.

Each circle represents a pulse beat, and each row of circles is to be clapped around continuously. This means that the final beat in the row should be thought of as falling right before the first beat of the same row, so that the pulse flows continuously from the end of the line back to the beginning. Experiment with different tempos (rates of pulse), but follow two basic guidelines: start slow and, once you've started try to maintain an even pulse, don't slow down or speed up. If you start slow and then wish to try the pulse exercise faster, stop and start again at a faster tempo.

Below is a simple pulse with no accentuation. Clap the pulse at a comfortable tempo. Note that you may naturally tend to group the pulse into twos or threes by creating strong and weak beats. Try to avoid this, and maintain as even a pulse as possible with no accentuation and no speeding or slowing.

Next, the pulse is grouped into twos by alternating stressed (black) and unstressed (white) circles. Clap at a slow tempo, repeating the pulse around and around several times. Then stop and clap at a quick rate, this time tapping your foot only on the stressed beats. You now have two pulses going—the quicker clapping pulse and the slower tapping pulse. This is the beginning of rhythm within a simple musical context. The faster pulse, with alternating stresses, may be considered a basic musical rhythm, while the tapping foot keeps the underlying beat (the slower pulse) at a comfortable physical tempo.

Now the pulse will be grouped into threes through stressed and unstressed pulse beats. Clap and tap this at different tempos—clapping the pulse with accents as shown, tapping your foot on only the stressed beats.

In the next example, the groupings that are created by the stressed beats are no longer regular. Although still a simple pulse, the accentuation is creating groupings of different lengths. This creates more interest and a stronger sense of motion. Try tapping your foot on every other pulse beat as you clap this rhythm. This can be very difficult, as one of the stressed beats falls in between foot taps. Try it first without the accents. When you're comfortable, begin to clap the accents. In this exercise, the foot is keeping the beat and the clapping is creating rhythm through accenting.

Next are some other pulses with irregular stresses. These may be played as individual rhythms, repeating over and over from the end of each line back to the beginning. You may also try playing through from the top line through each descending line to the last line and then back again to the top. Try clapping the pulse with just the accents first, then try tapping and clapping. Tap on every other pulse beat—maintaining a subdivision of two—as you clap all the beats, clapping harder on the stressed (filled in) circles as indicated. Notice how the visual representation of these pulse rhythms reflects the way design is a part of the musical concept. Some of the exercises may be very difficult to coordinate at first.

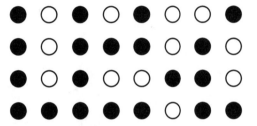

The example below has three levels of stress—black for the primary accent, gray indicating a secondary accent (accented, but not as strongly as for a black circle), and white for unaccented. The cycle created is a four-beat cycle: the first beat accented, the second unaccented, the third with a secondary accent, and the fourth unaccented. Try clapping this pulse rhythm at different tempos. Because the cycle is regular, containing four pulses or beats, this rhythm is again describing a time-measure (or simply a "measure") though a more involved one than the two- and three-beat measures from the earlier examples. The four-beat cycle is central to a great deal of musical rhythm.

Using varied shadings, as in the next examples, it is possible to create complex patterns of accentuation.

This method of visualizing is one way of writing down and communicating rhythmic ideas. It is a simple form of music notation. The more universally used form of rhythmic notation is a more complex and flexible system. Understanding notation is necessary for the operation of almost all drum machines and sequencers and will help you to create and play a much wider variety of beats and patterns.

## LEARNING RHYTHMS.

At first glance, this section title might not make a lot of sense. Many people feel that rhythmic skill is completely instinctive—something you either have or you don't.

Actually, this couldn't be much further from the truth. In psychological tests, infants have been shown to respond to tonal patterns in a way that is similar to the way they respond to spoken language. To be human is to be capable of making music, just as to be human is to be capable of speech.

As with language, the capacity to learn music changes as a child grows older. Tests show that the affinity for rhythmic development hits a peak when a child reaches the age of about eleven to twelve years old, and then it begins to taper off. It's true that people who receive training at early ages will tend to exhibit higher degrees of musical ability later in life. It's also true that a person with no formal training as a child, raised in a nonmusical or nonmovement-oriented environment, may struggle to learn to express rhythm when attempted at a later age. Nonetheless, as studies bear out, to be human is to be capable of music, and though it may be difficult at first to try to connect with some of the instinctive elements of rhythm, it is possible for anyone to attain a high level of rhythmic and musical ability at any age.

Initially, you're going to have to narrow your sights on the details and the basics of your craft, so that eventually you'll be able to communicate the broader range of emotion possible through music.

New technology and computer programs have provided a fast entry into the world of music for interested nonmusicians. This opening of doors is revolutionary in its potential for increasing music participation, yet it raises questions about the value and necessity of acquiring a basic knowledge of music. If you can program listenable music by pressing a few buttons, why take the time to bone up on old-fashioned skills that may soon become obsolete? There are several reasons.

Learning to use a sequencer without ever learning various types of rhythm combinations will limit the range of music you'll be able to perform or program. Chances are you'll end up programming only as much music as you have in your own memory bank. To increase your rhythm vocabulary, it's well worth exploring the drum beats and styles that are currently in use. Knowledge of the physical act of drumming is also helpful. Although you can set up sequencer rhythms without the ability to keep a beat, having knowledge of musical coordination and the way drummers work and think will greatly enhance your ability to evolve and humanize your patterns. Keeping the beat is a natural part of our musical sense and needs to be developed by anyone participating in the creation of music, whether on acoustic or electronic instruments.

At its best, music can express the full range of human emotional and intellectual capabilities, yet the process of learning music and musicianship can be as repetitive, mundane, and downright boring as any human endeavor. Initially, you're going to have to narrow your sights on the details and the basics of your craft, so that eventually you'll be able to communicate the broader range of emotion possible through music. The ultimate pay-off is definitely worth the effort.

# CHAPTER 2

# Written Rhythm: Notation and Design

Notation is the universal
language of music,
and it is a tremendous
aid in organizing and
retaining musical ideas,
communicating with
other musicians, and
programming sequencers,
samplers, and drum
machines.

Today more than ever, there is wide-open opportunity for the untrained musician to get involved in pop music through the use of computer programs, keyboard synthesizers, samplers, drum machines, and various hybrids that incorporate all or many of these functions. Unfortunately, many people who might derive pleasure from musical expression are put off by the obstacle of learning musical notation. While a certain amount of musical creation can happen without an understanding of notation, it is very difficult to accomplish much without at least a basic understanding of the construction of music using the terms of notation. Ultimately, a complete understanding of notation is necessary for a complete facility with music and these new technological tools of music creation.

There are some valid reasons for "fear of notation," stemming largely from the actual limitations of the note-writing system. In the widely-used Suzuki method for teaching music to young children, the standard notational system is not used, at least not until students have acquired basic instrumental technique. The rationale is that notation may be an obstacle for beginners, young or old, because they can inevitably play and compose much more complex music than they can read or notate. Notation tends to draw note-readers away from the way music actually sounds because they are concentrating on the way it appears on paper; the brain tends not to tune into the ear if it's concentrating on the page.

Still, Suzuki appreciates the ultimate necessity of notation in facilitating the pursuit of music. It simply must be part of a balanced plan, and the importance of learning to read music far outweighs its temporary drawbacks. On the plus side, reading music is much easier to learn than playing a musical instrument. Once the system is understood—and it's not much more complicated than learning fractions of an apple or a pie as you did in elementary school—a basic working understanding can follow very quickly. Notation is the universal language of music, and it is a tremendous aid in organizing and retaining musical ideas, communicating with other musicians, and programming sequencers, samplers, and drum machines. Interestingly, while physical coordination is not strictly necessary for music programming, a basic understanding of notation is.

The following discussion deals with the basics of musical notation and simple rhythms. Most of you aren't eleven or twelve years old any more, so absorbing this information might be a little slow going at first. That's okay. Notation is a useful tool, but it's not the most important part of understanding, playing, or composing music.

It is not the intention of this book to train the reader to become fluent in written music. Fluency takes a lot of time to develop and is generally unnecessary in performing most popular music. What you'll find in this section is only as much notation as is necessary to cover the basic kind of rhythms used in today's pop music—the same rhythms you may want to use as the basis for your own playing or programming. Those of you already familiar with written music may want to skim this chapter and the next, trying the rhythms and refreshing your memory of certain concepts such as meter and syncopation. Those who have never learned to read music, or have only a scant understanding of written music, should probably take your time sifting through this material.

Visualizing rhythms, thinking of them as designs or patterns, is another useful method of understanding and a valuable adjunct to the notational system. The pulse game from the previous chapter is a good example of the way rhythms may be visually represented. The design aspect of rhythm will be pointed out in some of the following discussions.

Bear in mind that this chapter deals only with the rhythmic side of notation and doesn't touch on melody or harmony. For more complete discussions of notation refer to any introductory music text.

Despite Plato's observation that rhythm is "an order of movement," the rhythmic order in some musical compositions may be very difficult to find. In most pieces of music, these include the basic elements of beat, tempo, measure, meter, and phrase, as well as the broader concepts of structure and style.

The modern system of notation uses a variety of symbols to represent musical events in time—Plato's order of movement. The basic system is quite simple, using a relatively small number of symbols to represent musical events. Once you have familiarized yourself with the symbols, along with a few basic principles, most commonly used rhythms will be easily under-stood.

Musical symbols, aside from indicating pitch, represent relative durations of time. These relative durations of time are expressed as fractions, just as a pie can be separated into fractional parts. The whole note is the largest unit of rhythm, with shorter durations of time expressed as fractions of the whole note. These shorter units are called half note, quarter note, eighth note, sixteenth note, and so on. Each of these notes has its own symbol. A half note adds a stem to a whole note, and a quarter note darkens in the head of the half note. An eighth note adds a flag to a quarter note with flags added on as the value of the notes decreases by half.

Notes are written on a musical staff, which consists of five lines and four spaces:

A musical note indicates a musical sound, and for each note there is an equivalent rest indicating a relatively equal amount of silence. The next page shows the symbols used for the notes and the rests.

Rhythm is primarily the process of dividing up time, and these symbols give us a simple way of representing these relative lengths of time.

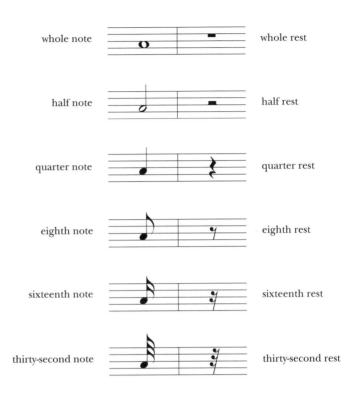

| | |
|---|---|
| whole note | whole rest |
| half note | half rest |
| quarter note | quarter rest |
| eighth note | eighth rest |
| sixteenth note | sixteenth rest |
| thirty-second note | thirty-second rest |

Notes with flags on the stems may be grouped together using beams instead of flags. Beams provide a simplified visual approach to the writing of complicated rhythms.

Next are shown the relative values of notes and rests, indicating their basic fractional relationship (one whole note equals two half notes which equals four quarter notes, and so on).

These notes and rests are the basis of the entire notational system. Rhythm is primarily the process of dividing up time, and these symbols give us a simple way of representing these relative lengths of time. The development of the notational system will correspond to the development of rhythm in music.

## PULSE + TEMPO = BEAT

As we saw in the previous chapter, pulse is the underlying, regular beat present in almost all rhythms. As a basic unit it may be represented by repeated notes of any single given value.

A repeating pulse at a given tempo creates the beat. Popular use has blurred the exact meanings of these terms, and you may hear the beat of a song referred to as its pulse, its tempo, or its beat.

Tempo is the rate of the pulses, meaning the amount of time between each pulse beat. A repeating pulse at a given tempo creates the beat. Popular use has blurred the exact meanings of these terms, and you may hear the beat of a song referred to as its pulse, its tempo, or its beat.

The beat remains constant throughout most pieces of popular music. Beat is loosely defined as the rhythmic unit one responds to in dancing or walking. The beat is primarily what ties music to human movement. Tempos are assigned to the beat, and these are shown on paper or on screen with tempo marks or metronome indications. Tempo marks are tempo instructions usually given in their Italian form (e.g., adagio, allegro) and are general indications that allow room for interpretation. Metronome tempos are given relative to note values such as ♩ = 76, indicating that the tempo of the quarter note is seventy-six beats per minute. Sequencers use this metronomic number system for defining the tempo of the rhythm. In live popular music, the tempo, or the beat, is usually established by simply "counting in."

Rhythm emerges from patterns of sounds and silences. These patterns are set up relative to a consistent pulse and tempo. The relative value of the notes also remains consistent. Thus in the example following, the eighth notes will be played twice as rapidly as the preceding quarter notes, no matter what the starting tempo.

As you can see, the entire notational system is built on relative values. The notes are first relative to the beat and then relative to each other based on their fractional values. In order to make this system work, we must assign a note value to the beat. We accomplish this, and also provide a simple to organize the beats, via the time signature.

## GROUPING BEATS—TIME SIGNATURES.

**It simplifies matters to organize the beats of a piece of music into small groups of equal size, called bars or measures.**

It simplifies matters to organize the beats of a piece of music into small groups of equal size, called bars or measures. Measures are separated by bar lines, which are vertical lines through the staff. The number of beats in each measure is constant. (There might be four in each measure, for example.) The time signature, which appears at the beginning of a piece of written music, describes the number of beats in each measure as follows:

top number = number of beats in a measure

bottom number = note value of each beat

The most common time signature is $\frac{4}{4}$ (called "four-four time"), which indicates that there are four beats to the measure (top number) and that each beat is given the value of one quarter note (bottom number). The bottom number is understood to be the bottom of a fraction, thus the bottom 4 in $\frac{4}{4}$ time is read as $\frac{1}{4}$, meaning that a quarter note is being assigned the value of the beat.

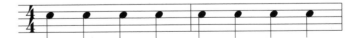

In $\frac{3}{4}$ time, there are three beats to the measure, and the beat is again assigned the value of one quarter note.

In $\frac{6}{8}$ time the beat is now assigned the value of one eighth note and there are six of them in each measure.

The bottom number in a time signature must be a multiple of two in order to represent a note value (usually a four or eight, meaning a quarter or an eighth note.)

Rhythms are created using various values of notes and rests within a time signature. The rhythms work relative to the beat and must maintain the correct number of beats in each measure. This means that the total value of the notes and rests in any given measure must equal the value and number of beats indicated in the time signature. Thus, in any measure of $\frac{4}{4}$ time, the notes and rests must add up to four quarter notes' worth of time.

The last measure of the example below contains a $\frac{4}{4}$ time pattern made up of one quarter note, an eighth-note rest, three eighth notes, and then a quarter note. Added together these values equal four quarter notes' worth of time or one measure of $\frac{4}{4}$, as with each of the measures in this example.

The following examples show various simple rhythms in different time signatures. Notice how the values of the notes and rests in each measure add up to the value indicated by the time signature. Notice also that the beams provide a visual aid in identifying individual beats. In general, the physical layout of these rhythms illustrates the nature of design in rhythm notation. Each beat occupies roughly the same physical space (as does each measure), with half notes twice as far from each other as the quarter notes, the quarter notes twice as far as the eighth notes, and so on. Though notation does not require that music be written this way (and it often isn't, given the space limitation of manuscript paper), it does help us visualize the underlying beats of each measure. We will maintain this visual aid in the way rhythms are written throughout this book.

Once you are clear on the meaning and relationship of notes, rests, and time signatures, you have grasped the essence of the entire system of written rhythm.

This completes our discussion of the essentials of rhythm notation. Once you are clear on the meaning and relationship of notes, rests, and time signatures, you have grasped the essence of the entire system of written rhythm.

## METER AND THE FOUR-BEAT CYCLE.

Time signatures reflect the natural tendency to create music in repetitive cycles of beats. The most common grouping is that of four beats or four-four time, also called the four-beat cycle. In almost all world cultures, the four-beat cycle is the predominant beat cycle. Two- and three-beat cycles are also common, but the four-beat cycle has apparently developed on its own in most musical cultures. Just as music itself is innately human in a way only vaguely understood, the four-beat cycle seems to be an innate preference within the musical language.

Like so many other musical rules, meter can be followed, bent, played with, or ignored in order to produce a musical effect.

Meter, on the other hand, is not nearly as universal as the four-beat cycle. Meter refers to the underlying feeling of accentuation that normally accompanies a time signature. This is a very important rhythmic concept. It is saying that in each beat cycle or measure, there are degrees of accent that are felt and subtly translated into our playing of each individual beat. Certain accenting patterns occur naturally and become standard practice. Like so many other musical rules, meter can be followed, bent, played with, or ignored in order to produce a musical effect. World cultures vary widely in the patterns of accents that they apply to the four-beat cycle. In the rhythm of popular music, the meter or underlying accentuation of the four-beat cycle has its own distinctive pattern.

Meter in the Western classical tradition is expressed in terms of accents, secondary accents, and unaccented notes. The classical $\frac{4}{4}$ meter, which differs from the meter you'll find in pop music, is indicated below with a slash indicating an accent, a dash indicating a secondary accent, and a U indicating an unaccented note.

/ = primary accent
— = secondary accent
U = unaccented

In this instance, it is the 3-beat, the secondary accent, that distinguishes the four-beat cycle from two successive two-beat cycles. If the 3-beat were a primary accent, this would be a two-beat meter cycle. It is the secondary accent that creates the four-beat cycle.

The following chart shows the standard meter in all of the common time signatures used in the Western classical tradition. Simple meter includes groupings by two, three, and four. Compound meter multiplies each of these by three; giving six, nine, and twelve. You should approach all of your rhythm playing with an awareness of possible underlying feelings of accentuation. Meter represents an important bridge to the subtlety of rhythmic expression.

| TIME SIGNATURE | | | METER |
|---|---|---|---|
| $\frac{2}{2}$ | $\frac{2}{4}$ | $\frac{2}{8}$ | simple duple<br>/ U<br>1 2 |
| $\frac{3}{2}$ | $\frac{3}{4}$ | $\frac{3}{8}$ | simple triple<br>/ U U<br>1 2 3 |
| $\frac{4}{2}$ | $\frac{4}{4}$ | $\frac{4}{8}$ | simple quadruple<br>/ U — U<br>1 2 3 4 |
| $\frac{6}{2}$ | $\frac{6}{4}$ | $\frac{6}{8}$ | compound duple<br>/ U U — U U<br>1 2 3 4 5 6 |
| $\frac{9}{2}$ | $\frac{9}{4}$ | $\frac{9}{8}$ | compound triple<br>/ U U — U U — U U<br>1 2 3 4 5 6 7 8 9 |
| $\frac{12}{2}$ | $\frac{12}{4}$ | $\frac{12}{8}$ | compound quadruple<br>/ U U — U U — U U — U U<br>1 2 3 4 5 6 7 8 9 10 11 12 |

# CHAPTER 3

# Practice Rhythms

**W**ith the basics of rhythm notation under your belt, some simple practice rhythms will help you learn the essential building blocks of many popular rhythms. The best way to approach the following examples is to tap your foot as you clap the rhythm. Begin by tapping your foot with authority until it becomes second nature. Then clap the given rhythms or play them on an instrument. If you have had little or no musical training, this might at first seem a little like rubbing your stomach and tapping your head at the same time, but it is pretty simple once you get the hang of it. It's important that you maintain this tapping of your foot because this underlying pulse is the foundation of almost all rhythm.

## EIGHT-NOTE RHYTHMS

Below is a measure of $\frac{4}{4}$ time consisting of an eighth-note pulse. The beat, as defined by the time signature, is a quarter note with four quarter notes per measure. In this rhythm, we have subdivided each beat into two notes, with two eighth notes equaling one quarter note and eight eighth notes adding up to a complete measure of $\frac{4}{4}$.

When repeating or cycling these rhythms, the pulse or beat should flow directly from the final beat of the final measure back into the first beat of the first measure, maintaining a nonstop and even pulse.

An easy way to count this rhythm is to assign a name to each note. The beats (often distinguished more precisely as *primary* beats) are labeled 1, 2, 3, and 4. The in-between notes, created by our subdivision into eighth notes, are labeled as *and* beats.

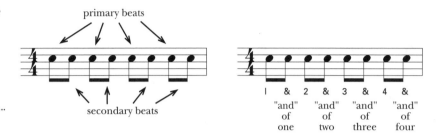

Notice the way the beams (indicating eighth notes) are used. The 1-beat is beamed to the following *and* beat, the 2-beat to the next *and* beat, and so on. This shows the organization of beats. The *and* beat following beat 1 is linked with beat 1 (it's connected by a beam, if the rhythm allows) and is correctly termed the "and" of 1. (As we progress through various rhythms, be aware of how we use beams to maintain a visual sense of notes that are within the same beat. The use of beams is a great aid in reading rhythms because of the way it allows you to see each independent beat.) Although this example is a simple pulse, it is also a rhythm, and you should tap and clap it. Tap your foot on the numbers only; clap on all eight beats. It's helpful to keep track of each note name as you go, counting 1 *and* 2 *and* 3 *and* 4 *and*.

The following examples are in various time signatures and use the eighth note as the smallest subdivision. The rhythms should be repeated around and around many times. When repeating or cycling these rhythms, the pulse or beat should flow directly from the final beat of the final measure back into the first beat of the first measure, maintaining a nonstop and even pulse.

Try creating your own eighth-note rhythms following these examples. You might approach this in two different ways. First, start by imagining the beat alone. Then add a rhythm by filling in certain notes either on the beat or on the eighth note following each beat. Second, start off with the eighth note pulse used at the beginning of this section. Variations may be created by omitting any number of the notes in the pulse. Both ways of thinking about rhythm—as filling an empty space or as making space in a continuous pulse—are valid, and each can suggest different and interesting ideas.

When performing these rhythms, remember that it is better to mess up the rhythm and maintain the beat than to lose the beat in trying to stay with the rhythm. If you fumble the pattern, just let the beat keep coming around to one and try again until you can clap the rhythm correctly over the tapping foot.

A metronome can help to reinforce the beat, but don't rely on it to replace the tapping of the foot. You've got to keep the beat. It's a good idea to keep mental track of the count as you clap and tap (for example, repeat to yourself "1, 2, 3, 4, 1, 2, 3, 4," in $\frac{4}{4}$). It is also fun to experiment with tempos from slow to fast (sometimes it's harder to play really slow than really fast), and a metronome can help establish the various tempos. Remember that coordination takes repeated practice, but once it's mastered it becomes second nature. Rhythm is in all of us — we must simply help it to the surface.

## THE CURVED LINE—TIES

The curved line has a variety of uses in music notation, but it serves most often as a tie. A tie joins two notes together to create a longer note. Thus the two tied quarter notes below are equal to one half note.

The tie is useful when a sound is to be sustained over a bar line. For example:

The tie is also used to maintain a visual reminder of the placement of the beat, similar to the way beams are used. The following two rhythms sound identical. One is written with beams and ties, the other with varying note values. While it is important to become familiar with the second kind of notation, the first kind is easier to read: we can *see* where the beats occur.

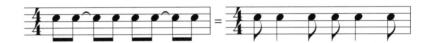

## SYNCOPATION

Syncopation is a rhythmic term that is often misused or misunderstood. Broadly defined, syncopation is any abnormality in meter. In practice, this translates into the absence of an accent on a normally accented beat (as defined by the meter) or an accent on a normally unaccented beat. Another definition calls syncopation a lack of coincidence between the rhythm and the beat. Syncopation is so broadly applied in all forms of contemporary music—popular and classical—that the term is only really useful in discussing degrees of syncopation, or the degree to which the rhythm varies from the meter and/or the beat.

A very basic syncopation is shown below. On the left is simple 4-meter, showing primary and secondary accents. On the right, the rhythm leaves out beat 3, defined in classical meter as a secondary accent, and thus creates a syncopation. This also conforms to the idea of a temporary lack of coincidence between the rhythm and the beat—the rhythm here does not play on beat 3, meaning they don't coincide.

In the next example of syncopation, written both with ties and without, we use an eighth-note subdivision to create a more syncopated feeling.

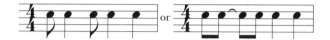

Here the syncopation is created by the absence of beat 2, but the degree of syncopation is greater than in the previous example because of the *and* beats which are played before and after the missing 2 beat. Here we are led from beat 1 to beat 2 by the *and* of 1 but, instead of landing on the 2, we skip over it, picking up at the *and* of 2 and finally resolving back to the beat at beat 3. This is a common and important kind of syncopation in all forms of popular music. It can be difficult to master in clapping and tapping, but the result is worth the effort. Part of the advantage of learning rhythm by clapping and tapping is that in a case such as this, the missing 2 beat is played by the tapping foot. Try it on the next rhythm, a pattern commonly found in the underlying rhythm of many popular songs. This is similar to the previous example except that in the first measure it leaves out both the 2- and the 3-beats, finally resolving on beat 4. Syncopation often excludes more than one of the primary beats in a measure.

In the following two-measure rhythms, you hear this basic type of syncopation applied in various ways. As rhythms become more removed from the beat, they also become more difficult to read and to coordinate. Some of the rhythms below are written using beams and ties. Others are written using notes of whatever length necessary to create the desired rhythm. Though this second style of writing may be initially more difficult to read, it has become the more commonly accepted practice.

Notice that in the final two-measure example you play on the 1-beat of measure 1 and then play only the *and* beats through the rest of measure 1 and throughout measure 2. This rhythm suggests what is called a *cross pulse*. A cross pulse is one that runs contrary to the beat in some manner. Cross pulses can be extended into polyrhythms, which we'll look at in a later chapter.

The one-measure rhythm below is a very common syncopated rhythm. Notice that the time from beat 1 to the *and* of beat 2 is one and one-half beats, or a quarter note plus an eighth note.

There is another symbol that is used in notation to create this length of note. A note with a dot following the note head— called a *dotted note*— indicates that the value of the note is extended by one half of the value of the note that is written. Thus, a dotted quarter note is equal to a quarter note plus an eighth note, a dotted half note is equal to a half note plus a quarter note, and so on. The dotted note is extremely common in written music. The rhythm above is rewritten here using the dotted quarter note.

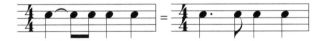

The equivalent note values for a dotted quarter note appears as follows:

A few basic rhythms using dotted notes follow:

In these more complex rhythms, correct use of the beams is very important to help keep track of the beat.

Sixteenth-note rhythms are created by dividing the quarter note beat into four equal parts or by dividing the eighth-note pulse in half. A sixteenth-note pulse in $\frac{4}{4}$ time would appear as follows:

Play this rhythm, getting a feel for groups of four to the beat, four beats to the bar. Remember to count the beat numbers to yourself (1, 2, 3, 4, and so on). Notice that each beat is isolated by beaming groups of four sixteenth notes. In these more complex rhythms, correct use of the beams is very important to help keep track of the beat.

The sixteenth note between a primary beat and an *and* beat is labeled as an *e* beat and the sixteenth note between an *and* beat and the following primary beat is an *a* beat as follows:

One interesting way of thinking about sixteenth notes is to isolate a single beat. There are various possibilities for altering the sixteenth note rhythm in one beat. The possibilities will consist of all four sixteenth notes being struck, three out of the four, two of the four, one of the four, or none of the four. Some of them are written below with the primary beats labeled as P (It may be helpful to repeat each example to yourself several times to let it sink in.)

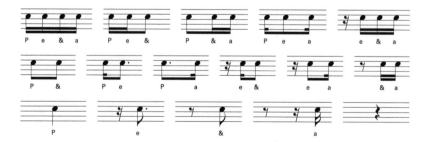

Stringing these beats together in various ways produces a tremendous variety of rhythms:

Create your own rhythms using sixteenth notes. Remember to repeat rhythms several time when clapping and tapping. Coordinating some of these rhythms can be very tricky at first, so take it slowly and don't be discouraged. It's like learning to ride a bicycle—difficult at first, but easier once you get the hang of it.

## TRIPLET RHYTHMS

You may have noticed that up to this point all the rhythmic division you've seen been in multiples of two. The fractional system of notes is based on twos—whole notes, half notes, quarters, eighths, and so on. You have seen groups of three beats in $\frac{3}{4}$ time, but so far we haven't dealt with a situation where beats themselves are divided in three. The notation system uses what is called a *triplet* to create groups of three evenly-spaced notes within a beat. Triplets are notated with a three above the note group, using a bracket if there are no beams. The standard note symbols are used, but as triplets their value is diminished to allow three to the beat—a mathematical impossibility that's used in music nonetheless. (e.g., three eighth note triplets is equal to two regular eighth notes.)

A measure of eighth-note triplets in $\frac{4}{4}$—three evenly spaced notes to the beat—would be labeled and appear as follows:

If you dissect groups of triplets in the same way you did sixteenth notes in the previous section, you can come up with numerous rhythmical possibilities using three, two, one, or no triplets in one quarter-note beat.

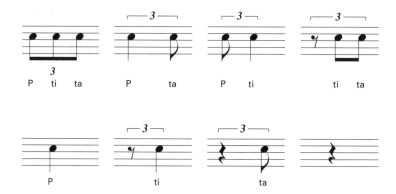

You may then create extended triplet rhythms by combining beats from the above possibilities. In the follwoing rhythms, notice that there is a tendency to rely on the first and third notes of the triplet (the primary beat and the "ta" beat). This combination of notes is called a shuffle, and it is used extensively in pop music and especially the blues. Notice that the triplet signs help to isolate the individual beats.

*The Rhythm Book*

Remember that rhythms don't always fall into the neat categories covered here. They may combine all of these approaches—including eighth notes, sixteenth notes, and triplets—in the space of a single measure.

Create your own triplet patterns and rhythms of all types. Remember that rhythms don't always fall into the neat categories covered here. They may combine all of these approaches - including eighth notes, sixteenth notes, and triplets —in the space of a single measure. Most popular music is created from simple combinations such as those you've been practicing so far, but rhythmic invention can stretch much further, and the possibilities are endless.

# CHAPTER 4

# Drums and Percussion

Before moving on to rhythms in pop music and the techniques of programming rhythm, it's a good idea to explore the instruments that have served as the traditional tools of drummers and percussionists and that continue to provide the basis for today's digitally-generated sounds.

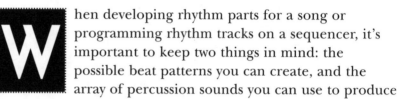

When developing rhythm parts for a song or programming rhythm tracks on a sequencer, it's important to keep two things in mind: the possible beat patterns you can create, and the array of percussion sounds you can use to produce the rhythms. The most important rhythm instrument in today's music is obviously the drum set, which is actually made up of several types of drums and cymbals. The drum set is used for the basic beats and rhythm patterns of popular music, but an ever increasing number of auxiliary instruments are being added to the modern song's collection of sounds, facilitating the production of a wide range of colors and effects. Many of these instruments are preprogrammed into the sound libraries of synthesizers and samplers. Before moving on to rhythms in pop music and the techniques of programming rhythm, it's a good idea to explore the instruments that have served as the traditional tools of drummers and percussionists and that continue to provide the basis for today's digitally-generated sounds. Drums are certainly among the oldest and most widespread of musical instruments. They exist in all parts of the world and come in a staggering number of shapes, sizes, and sounds. The current instruments of the percussion family, including many instruments other than drums, are the products of considerable cross-cultural development and refinement.

The instruments of the percussion family are generally classified into two basic categories: instruments of definite pitch such as the glockenspiel, xylophone, and kettledrum; and instruments of indefinite pitch such as the triangle, bass drum, and tambourine. The second group may be further broken down into hand percussion, meaning instruments held in the hand when played, and the more involved drums and cymbals which require stands or slings. For this discussion, we will divide the percussion family into four groups: pitched percussion instruments, hand percussion, drums and cymbals, and the modern drum set.

...the piano is considered by some to be a rhythm instrument because the striking of its keys is similar to the manner in which most percussion is played (as opposed to the bowing or blowing common to most other orchestral instruments).

The techniques for making rhythm are tremendously varied and involve the use of hands alone or of mallets and sticks. Hand technique may be used on our own bodies, as with "hambone" or certain children's games, or applied directly to a wide variety of instruments such as bongos or tambourine. In the most evolved technique, the use of hands on the Indian tabla drum employs a subtle array of gestures which can produce an amazing variety of sounds and pitches. Stick and mallet techniques also vary widely depending on the instrument being played. The military roll on a snare drum, for example, involves a sophisticated stick bouncing technique, while mallet use on the vibraphone, marimba, and related instruments has developed into a complex four-mallet method that allows for chording. We will look at some of these techniques while exploring individual instruments.

## PITCHED PERCUSSION INSTRUMENTS

Pitched percussion instruments, not surprisingly, are instruments capable of producing tones recognizable as pitches within the Western system of scales. There are two basic subdivisions within this category. The first is the timpani (often referred to as a kettle drum), which is a large drum played with mallets. The second is a family of instruments loosely based on the piano. While not technically a member of the percussion family, the piano is considered by some to be a rhythm instrument because the striking of its keys is similar to the manner in which most percussion is played (as opposed to the bowing or blowing common to most other orchestral instruments). The instruments based on the piano borrow its keyboard concept but are struck with sticks or mallets rather than with the hand or fingers. We could call these instruments, which include the vibraphone and the marimba, *mallet keyboards.* Other cultures use a variety of pitched percussion instruments such as the entenga drums of Uganda, the tabla from India, and the increasingly popular steel drums from Trinidad. These are all sometimes employed in the popular music of this country.

Timpani consist of a skin (drum head) stretched over a hollow metal shell that is in the shape of a half sphere. Modern timpani may substitute plastic drum heads for skin and fiberglass shells for copper. The size and resonance of the large shell (23" to 32" in diameter) produce a deep, booming tone that is considered pure enough to tune to specific pitches.

Tuning is done by tightening or loosening the drum head with screws placed around the rim, or by a pedal attachment which stretches the head more tightly when depressed. Timpani are played with a mallet made of a wood or a metal handle attached to a globular head that is generally made of felt—though for different effects wood, yarn, leather, plastic, or sponge may also be used.

A minimum of two timpani are used in most orchestras, and they are normally tuned to the tonic and dominant (the first and fifth pitches of the major or minor scale) in the key of the composition. In twentieth century classical music, the role of the timpani has widened, with three or more kettledrums often required, along with frequent changes of tuning during a performance. Timpani are most commonly used for rhythmic accentuation but are also called on to produce sound effects such as thunder. When used in popular music (and it doesn't happen often), timpani can supply quite dramatic accents to highlight or mark the arrival of a particular song section. The Beatles used them in this way to begin the chorus of their 1965 song "Every Little Thing."

Used in pop music quite a bit more frequently than timpani are mallet keyboard instruments: the marimba, the xylophone, and the vibraphone. They provide a light and airy sound that can serve as an effective replacement for keyboard parts in the right song. They can also supply a woody, rustic percussion effect that adds exotic spice to melodies, rhythm, or backing tracks (the Police achieved this effect with a marimba sound in "King of Pain"). These instruments consist of tone bars, made of wood or synthetic material, which are arranged in two rows corresponding to the chromatic scale, just like the white and black keys of the piano. The size and thickness of the tone bars determine the pitch of the note. Below each tone bar is a metal pipe that acts as a resonator. The resonators are tuned to the pitch of the tone bar. They amplify each note and give the tone color a deeper and richer quality.

The marimba is an African-based instrument that is played with mallets. It is used primarily for melodies, although chordal harmony can be produced by using two mallets at the same time or by employing the contemporary four-mallet approach (a difficult technique in which two mallets are held in each hand and are spread out or adjusted to different intervals to play chords). Once a marimba note is played, it decays rapidly. Limited variations in sustain can be achieved by altering the strength of the mallet attack and by muting the note with a free hand. More pronounced sustain can be produced by rapidly alternating mallet attacks on the desired note, resulting in a percussive sustain called *tremolo*.

The vibraphone (or vibes) is popular music's most common member of the mallet keyboard family. From the opening introduction of the Rolling Stones' "Under My Thumb" to the jazz stylings of Milt Jackson, Gary Burton, and Bobby Hutcherson, the vibraphone has long been enjoyed for its distinctive, soft, metallic sound. It differs from the marimba largely in its capacity to produce glowing, sustained notes. This effect is controlled with the use of a pedal that releases felt damping bars from the tone bars, producing sustain. Like the marimba, vibes have a resonator pipe below each tone bar to amplify and enhance the sound of the instrument. The vibraphone, however, also has a mechanical element within each resonator pipe, driven by a small motor attached to the instrument. The motor rotates the element within the resonator pipe, producing a vibrato effect (a minute fluctuation in pitch). The speed of the motor is usually variable, allowing for adjustment in the speed of the vibrato (hence the instrument's name). The combination of a percussive attack and control over sustain and vibrato has made the vibraphone a highly versatile and popular instrument.

Other instruments in the mallet keyboard family that use metal tone bars are the glockenspiel, celesta, orchestra bells, and bell lyra. These are smaller and more primitive instruments than the vibes, having no pedal control over sustain and using either a simple resonator box or no resonators at all. They produce beautifully clear and sustained tones that are appropriate for certain types of music and musical passages. The glockenspiel is well-suited for doubling melody lines, and if you own or obtain a synthesizer or sampler that can produce this sound, you might try to bolster a melody by playing it on the glockenspiel in addition to the original instrument or voice. Bruce Springsteen supposedly stumbled across this technique around the time he was recording the album *Born To Run*, and he has used the sound in songs like "Thunder Road" and "Born to Run," and in his live performances. The celesta is an instrument that has the appearance of a very small piano and is sounded by playing a keyboard. Classical music buffs know of the celesta from its use in "Dance of the Sugar-Plum Fairy," in Tchaikovsky's *Nutcracker Suite*. Another related orchestral instrument is the chimes, essentially a string of resonator pipes which hang and are struck with a leather mallet, producing long, shimmering tones, tuned chromatically to specific pitches. They are often used in jazz or fusion music to add exotic sound effects.

We now turn to instruments described as having indefinite pitch. This doesn't mean that these instruments have no pitch at all, simply that the pitch produced is too complex to categorize within the standard system of scale tones. These instruments do, in fact, have pitch in the sense of sound qualities that can be heard as relatively high or low. The concept of relative pitch is very important in the use of all percussion instruments and has an effect on the way we assign specific rhythm parts to particular drums.

## HAND PERCUSSION

Hand percussion could really include thousands of instruments, encompassing "found" objects and everyday tools like spoons and pots, along with traditional instruments such as cowbells and washboards. Multipercussionists in Latin, jazz and world music have elevated the playing of hand percussion to a high art, using a dazzling array of instruments to create infinite shades of musical color. Most popular music, however, draws from a basic collection of hand percussion that includes several traditional Latin-American and African-derived instruments. The following discussion will touch on those instruments that are used most frequently: the triangle, wood block, castanets, whistles, cowbell, claves, tambourine, guiro, maracas and other rattles, and cabasa.

The triangle and the wood block are the simplest forms of hand percussion. The triangle is a simple steel bar, bent in the shape of a triangle and struck with a steel rod. It's suspended from a hook that it will vibrate freely and produce a high, tinkling sound of indefinite pitch. The wood block is a small block of wood with a thin hollow part just below the top surface that acts as a resonator. The block is struck with a wooden stick to produce a sharp, clacking sound, somewhat like the clopping of horses' hooves. Striking the wood block in different places using either the tip or the side of the stick will produce slight variations in the sound. Castanets have been widely used by Spanish dancers performing to Flamenco dance music. They consist of two shell-shaped pieces of hard wood which are hinged together with string at their base. The string is looped around the thumb and forefinger of the player's hand, allowing the shells to be opened and closed so that they produce a clacking sound. By playing one in each hand, a skillful player of the castanets can produce very rapid and intricate rhythms. Modern orchestral castanets have springs and handles which facilitate playing but eliminate the accuracy of rhythm that is obtainable with the traditional castanets.

Whistles are used primarily for sound effects, though often the effect is meant for a precise rhythmic location and duration. Some of the sound effects possible from various whistles include birdcalls, sirens, wind sounds, cyclones, and tugboat and train whistles. A whistle may also refer to a small endblown flute made of wood, metal, or plastic with six finger holes. Some Brazilian music uses whistles in the context of street samba percussion ensembles.

The cowbell is a metal instrument that has evolved from several sources and is now part of the ever-growing percussion arsenal included in many drum machines. The most traditional type of cowbell contains a clapper and produces a clamorous sound ideally suited to its original use, which was to keep track of the movement of cattle. More recent English and American bells are tuned to definite pitch and are rung in succession to create simple melodies. Today's most commonly used cowbell does not have a clapper and is played with a stick. Like the wood block, the cowbell can produce different sounds depending on where it is struck: at the open end a low tone is sounded; at the closed end a higher tone is sounded. The volume and piercing quality of the cowbell make it best suited for simple repetitive rhythms, along the lines of its use in the classic Chambers Brothers song "Time Has Come Today." The cowbell is very common in Latin-America music and Latin-influenced pop tunes.

The word claves in Spanish means key to a code or keystone of an arch, which gives some indication of the importance of this percussion instrument in Latin music. It has also crept into rock music: the Beatles, for example, used it prominently in their 1964 hit "And I Love Her." The clave are two cylindrical pieces of hardwood that are struck together, producing a very sharp clacking sound with almost no sustain. The clave sound is often imitated on the drum set, using a technique called *cross-sticking* in which the back end of the drum stick is hit against the rim of the snare drum. This related sound is also included on most popular samples drum sets under the label *rim*.

The word tambourine is derived from the French word for drum, *tambour*. The tambourine is, in fact, a shallow drum, with skin stretched across one side and small metal plates (jingles) attached to the rim. In popular use, the tambourine is played much more in the manner of various hand percussion instruments than it is as a drum, with the jingles the predominant aspect of the instrument and the drum head often not played. Most tambourines used in pop music omit the head. The tambourine is often shaken to create a continuous sound, with accents added by tapping on the fist, elbow, or knee. A tambourine with a head may also be played primarily as a drum, with the jingles providing a secondary sound. Intricate patterns can be produced by alternating thumb and fingers on the hand. The tambourine is especially prevalent in Brazilian music, and it is one of the most widely used percussion instruments in popular music.

A guiro, or scraper, is generally made from a gourd with ribbing carved over most of the outer body. A stick is run over the ribbing producing a scratching sound, with the gourd acting as a resonator. The duration of the sound can be controlled by the length and speed of the hand stroke. The guiro is common in traditional Latin-American and Latin-influenced popular music. The washboard can serve as another kind of scraper and is still used in traditional New Orleans zydeco music, worn hung across the chest and played with both hands.

Maracas are the most common form of a very large class of hand percussion generally described as rattles or shakers. As with the tambourine, rattles are shaken to produce a continuous sound, sometimes accented so that a rhythmic pattern is created. Maracas are dried gourds with a handle, filled with dry seeds or shot. Another kind of common rattle is made from metal tubes filled with pebbles. The sound of a rattle or shaker is frequently included in the library of sounds on sampled drum sets.

A cabasa is sort of a combination of a rattle and a guiro. It is a round gourd rattle with ribbed sides, encased in a network of metal, pebbles, or plastic beads. The case of beads is generally held in one hand while the handle of the gourd (or wooden gourd substitute) is held in the other. The beads are scraped and rattled against the gourd with a circular motion of the wrist. Large gourds encased in beads are common in African music and are played by altering the manner of rotating the beads against the gourd, which sometimes includes throwing the gourd rhythmically.

*The cabasa*

©PHOTO BY MARTIN COHEN/LP MUSIC

There are many other types of hand percussion. Some of them, such as sleigh bells, slapsticks, ratchets, and even anvils, are used to create special sound effects. Still others are wholly human instruments" and include hand clapping, finger snapping, patting knees, stamping or scraping feet, and vocal sounds such as grunts, shouts, and breaks in the voice. Hand clapping has become quite widespread in popular music, as evidenced by its inclusion in the sound libraries of most sampled drum sets. All of these percussion instruments can add depth, color, and variety to drum beats and rhythm tracks and are well worth using in either their real or digital form.

Drums and cymbals, whether used separately or in combination as a drum set, are the central tools of rhythm in most of the world's music and especially in popular music. Drums have been fashioned into innumerable forms, from makeshift pots to elaborate works of art. The common elements in all drums are the hollow cylinder and the drum head or skin. Drums may have heads on one or both sides, the heads may be tunable (by varying the tautness of the skin over the cylinder), and they may be played either with the hands or with sticks of all different sizes and materials. Cymbals are generally large, circular, primarily brass plates that are also manufactured or built in various sizes with many different types of sound. They may be struck against each other or played with a stick or sticks. The most commonly used drums and cymbals are the subject of the following discussion.

Bongo and conga drums are probably the most widely used hand drums in the Western hemisphere and are associated particularly with Latin music. (The name conga comes from a Latin dance that was popularized in the United States in the Forties.) These one-headed drums are either held between the knees (bongos) or placed on the floor (congas). Conga drums are usually played in sets of two, providing a lower and a higher pitch that can generate two-voiced rhythms. Greater tonal variety may be achieved by using additional drums. Three sizes of congas are generally sold today: the tumba (largest size, lowest pitch), the conga (medium size, with the name used generically as well as for this specific sized drum), and the quinta (smallest size, highest pitch).

*Congas*

An enormous number of sounds and pitches may be coaxed from the head of a conga drum. The position of the hand on the drum as well as the shape and part of the hand used e.g., cupped hand, the palm, the palm and forefinger, the base of the palm) will affect the timbre and the pitch of the sound. A *portamento* (a sliding shift of pitch) effect can be created by sliding or pushing the thumb of one hand across the head while striking the head with the other hand. Conga drum heads are usually tunable via screws placed around the rim, though more primitive drums with permanently attached heads are tuned by heating and thus stretching the head.

The tom-tom falls into the largest class of drums used in the West. The name tom-tom is derived from the Hindi (Indian) tamtam, meaning drum, and has been used to describe American Indian and Oriental drums. Although still defined in Webster's as a hand drum, in current use tom-toms refer to a wide variety of drums that are almost always struck with sticks or mallets. The cylinder of the drum may be made from different types of hard wood, various metal alloys, fiberglass, or other modern synthetic materials. Tom-toms may have one head or two, and the heads are almost always tunable via screws placed around the rim holding the head to the cylinder. The second or bottom head acts as an additional resonator and gives the tom-tom a fuller, rounder sound. Tom-toms are usually found in groups of two or more, varying in diameter, depth, and relative pitch. The tom-toms used in the contemporary drum set are generally of the two-head variety, whereas concert toms (used with an orchestra) have only one head.

Timbales are a high-pitched form of tom-tom with one head. They have a metal shell and are usually played in a pair. Their distinctive sound is created by playing rim shots (using a drum stick to simultaneously strike the rim and the head of the drum), and they are also commonly played on the side of the metal cylinder for a clave-type sound. Timbales are most often used in Latin-American music.

The snare drum is very much in evidence in current pop music, most often providing a repeating "backbeat" accent that adds tension and interest to the main rhythm. Essentially a kind of tom-tom, the snare drum is a two-head drum with metal, nylon, or catgut strings (called snares) stretched tightly across the bottom head. When the top drum head is struck with a stick, the snares vibrate in response, producing a distinctive buzzing or rattling sound. The snare drum also has a release mechanism frees the snares from the bottom head, allowing the drum to sound like a basic tom-tom.

The snare drum originated as a marching drum used to accompany foot soldiers into battle during the Revolutionary and Civil Wars. It still plays a central role in the parade drumming tradition. In this military/marching band context, the snare drum is usually played suspended from the drummer's side. The most common current use of the snare however is within the drum set, where it is placed on a stand.

Stick technique on this drum is especially complex, in part because the buzzing of the snares serves to stretch out or sustain the sound. Certain playing techniques, originally used in the military, allow for unique special effects. One of these is the *military roll*, which is carried out by rapidly bouncing the two sticks in alternation on the top head of the drum. The quickly repeating beats generate a continuous buzzing sound from the snares.

A standard set of snare drum rudiments was developed in the Thirties, and they are still used today in elementary drum education. There are thirteen standard drum rudiments and a total of twenty-six rudiments in the basic approach to the snare drum. The rudiments include various basic rolls and alternating stick combinations such as the five- and seven-stroke rolls. Other rudiments have names that suggest their sound on their required hand movement, as in the following examples.

By combining various rudiments, the drummer can create many different sounds and rhythms, most of which we recognize from the military drum tradition. Some of these rudiments, especially the flam (which is really just an added grace note) are also common in popular drum set rhythms. The slurs created in the drag or ruff, in which several grace notes (created by bouncing the stick) precede an accented note, are also common in popular technique. Although the bounces are distinct in number (two in a drag, three in a four-stroke ruff, and so on) the effect is the same: a continuous rattle of the snares preceding the struck note. It is a sound which is unique to the snare drum.

Tenor drums and bass drums are larger members of the tom-tom family. Both are used in parade drumming and are generally suspended from the body with straps and played with sticks or mallets. The bass drum is carried upright and struck on both sides with mallets in either hand. Both of these instruments have been adapted to the drum set, with the tenor drum put on legs and called the floor tom, and the bass drum placed upright on the floor and played with a foot pedal.

Cymbals offer a bright contrast to the sound of drums, and in the context of rock and pop rhythms they've been put to a number of uses. In general, cymbals consist of large circular plates, usually made from a predominantly brass alloy. They are made in a very wide variety of sizes and shapes, from very large and heavy gongs that are struck with mallets to small finger cymbals that are played similarly to castanets. Most cymbals are quite thin and range from 10" to 24" in diameter. In the more traditional methods of performance, cymbals are played in pairs of equal-sized plates, with straps attached to the center of the cymbals so they may be held and struck together, producing a clashing sound. Cymbals may also be suspended individually and struck with a variety of types of sticks. In a drum set they are placed in numerous positions, on floor stands and holders that are attached to certain drums.

Stick technique, meaning the grip and manipulation of the drum sticks or mallets, varies depending on the style of music and the type of instrument you're playing. The basic technique involves holding the stick between the end of the thumb and the first joint of the forefinger, with the back of the stick running across the palm. This is similar to the way we would hold a hammer, except that the thumb is held against the stick rather than around it. The stick may also be held more loosely, with the play of the stick in the hand controlled by the ring and pinky fingers. The degree of play in the stick, as well as the position and tightness of the grip, will differ according to the musical style. In the last few decades, some drummers have developed quite intricate finger techniques that allow for very rapid rhythms and grace notes.

Traditional military drumming requires a different grip for the left hand stick. This traditional grip has the stick held at the base of the left-hand thumb and forefinger with the end of the stick protruding through the fingers, much as we normally hold a pen or pencil but with the wrist held up rather than down. This grip allows easy access to a drum when it is hanging at an angle from the side of a marching drummer.

A *matched grip* is one in which both hands are using the hammer type of grip described previously. It is the most widely used stick grip in today's music because of its application to the drum set, which has eclipsed the marching/military drum tradition. The matched grip is also used with orchestra percussion and mallet percussion instruments.

## THE DRUM SET

**The modern drum set is a marvel of ingenuity and practicality.**

The modern drum set is a marvel of ingenuity and practicality. It draws together a number of percussion instruments and borrows a basic structural concept from the piano: that the feet as well as the hands can be used to expand the musician's control of the instrument. By adding foot pedals to a practical configuration of assorted drums and cymbals, it brings to the single player the ability to produce many simultaneous rhythms and varying sound qualities. Its usefulness and range have made it the central percussion instrument in popular music.

The drum set evolved over several decades and was made possible in part by manufacturing techniques developed around the turn of the century. The invention of the bass drum pedal by George Olney in 1887 provided an initial mechanical breakthrough. It transferred from the hands to the feet the act of striking the bass drum with a mallet and thus freed the hands for other drum or percussion tasks.

A similar result was achieved by the development of the hi-hat, a vital component of the modern drum set. The hi-hat consists of a stand and foot pedal with two cymbals attached. The cymbals are facing each other in the manner of orchestra or parade cymbals that are struck together. By pressing the foot pedal, the drummer can cause the cymbals to strike each other, thus accomplishing a musical task that at one time had required two hands.

The height of the cymbals makes it possible to play them with sticks, which can be done while the cymbals are open or closed. In the open position, a splashy sustained sound is produced, the duration of which can be precisely controlled by altering the tension on the foot pedal or which can be choked off completely. In the closed position, a very clipped cymbal sound is produced, now widely used as the "ride" part of drum patterns. Open and closed hi-hat sounds are commonly included in the library of sounds on most sampled drum sets.

The hi-hat began as a hand-operated instrument that used a spring to close the cymbals together. It could be played with one hand, freeing the other hand to perform a different function. This instrument was used in the early twenties to accompany the Charleston, a popular dance of the time. The rhythm had a "boom/chick" sound produced by playing a rim shot on the drum on beat 1 followed by a cymbal clash on beat 2. This basic two-beat rhythm—a forerunner of the modern backbeat—could be performed by a single percussionist playing a rim shot with one hand and the hand-held cymbals with the other.

The first operation of two cymbals with a foot pedal accompanied the introduction of the low-hat, or lowboy, in 1923. The cymbals were low to the ground and had the appearance of a top hat, thereby inspiring the name. In 1928 Barney Walberg attached the low-hat to a thirty-two-inch tube, creating the modern hi-hat.

The name trap drums—a slang term for the drum set that is still in use—came from a shortening of the word contraptions.

Beginning around the turn of the century and continuing through the mid-twenties, makeshift drum sets were assembled by individual percussionists using all manner of assorted drum and percussion items. The demand for multi-percussion sounds came partly from vaudeville theater and the silent movies, which needed accompanying sound effects for the films and back-up drumming for the musical acts that performed while projectionists changed reels. The name trap drums—a slang term for the drum set that is still in use—came from a shortening of the word contraptions. (One can imagine a theater owner asking a percussionist to bring his "drums and contraptions" down to the theater to accompany the shows.)

By the thirties, the modern drum set had more or less settled into a standard combination of the two pedal instruments (the bass drum and the hi-hat), a snare drum on a stand, and a hanging cymbal (ride cymbal) placed on a stand so that it could be played with a stick. The addition of a tom-tom (or tom-toms) mounted on the bass drum and another tom-tom with legs placed on the floor (floor tom), completed the basic drum set as shown in the following photo:

*The drum set*

©PHOTO BY MARTIN COHEN/LP MUSIC

The basic concept of maintaining a pulse in one's strongest limb (right hand) and weakest limb (left foot) reflects the drummer's primary role as time-keeper.

This configuration has remained intact for the past half century. The only changes have focused on improvement of the pedal design and structural hardware and the addition and refinement of drums and cymbals. The most notable additions have been assorted tom-toms and hanging cymbals of different sizes and varieties.

The basic drum stick has also remained much the same over this period of time. The drum stick is 15" to 17" long, tapering to a beaded tip (modern drum stick tips are often nylon rather than wood, because they are more durable). Mallets and brushes (wire brushes on the end of sticks) are occasionally used to produce special effects.

The basic assignment of hands and feet to components of the drum set, for a right-handed person, is as follows: the right foot operates the bass drum pedal; the left foot operates the hi-hat pedal; the right hand uses a stick to play one of the hanging cymbals or the hi-hat cymbals; the left hand uses a stick to play the snare drum. The two hands also work together to create rolls, fills, and other breaks or short connecting rhythms, usually played on the snare drum and tom-toms.

Although the specifics of drum techniques may vary the fundamental idea is to create rhythms within the statement of the pulse. The individual components of the drum set have specific functions that support this concept. The hi-hat and ride cymbal are pulse-oriented, while the snare and bass drums are used for rhythm. If approached from the perspective of a right-handed drummer, the task of time-keeping is assigned to the strongest and weakest limbs (the right hand on the ride pattern and the left foot on the hi-hat pedal) and the rhythm function is carried out by the left hand on the snare and the right foot on the bass drum:

right hand = ride pattern (on cymbals) = pulse keeping

right foot = bass drum = downbeat + rhythm

left hand = snare drum = backbeat + rhythm

left foot = hit-hat pedal = slower pulse keeping

The basic concept of maintaining a pulse in one's strongest limb (right hand) and weakest limb (left foot) reflects the drummer's primary role as time-keeper.

The creation of rhythm patterns is now subject only to the whim, ear, and artistic judgment of the instrument user—the new rhythmist.

The logic by which instrument frequency ranges are matched to rhythmic function also seems to support the idea of the importance of the pulse. One of the pulse-keeping instruments is the hi-hat, which generates frequencies that are high enough to keep it out of the way of most other instruments and voices. The all-important downbeat, along with other fundamental points of rhythmic resolution, is sounded in the low frequency range of the bass drum, which also provides varying degrees of rhythmic development. The snare drum, operating in the middle frequencies, provides the backbeat, which is the fundamental rhythmic statement in most contemporary musical styles. The tom-toms, also in the middle frequencies, are used for embellishment and to fill in spaces allocated for rhythm statements. We can think of the high frequencies of the cymbals as providing a counterpoint to the low-sounding bass drum and the insistent backbeat of the snare.

These drumming procedures are meant only to provide a framework for understanding and are not to be taken as unbendable rules; sometimes the exceptions to the rules provide the most interesting and powerful musical statements. Within the more progressive offshoots of rock and roll, funk, and jazz, there are plenty of exceptions to the basic pulse-keeping or rhythm-making functions assigned to particular drums. Now, with the use of sequencers and samplers, the logic of drum set rhythm is no longer linked with physical dexterity and the assignment of strong limbs to prominent drum beats. The use of looped drum set samples is also changing the way drum patterns appear in popular music. The creation of rhythm patterns is now subject only to the whim, ear, and artistic judgment of the instrument user—the new rhythmist. Now, more than ever, that creative judgment needs a point of reference from which to move in new and innovative directions. It is only by examining the accepted practices in current pop music and its root forms that the creative drummer or programmer can make informed decisions about what possible new directions to take.

PART TWO

THE ROOTS OF MODERN RHYTHM

CHAPTER 5

# A Brief History of Rhythm

...in the final analysis, current music couldn't exist without the preparations of previous history and preceding music.

 hythm provides the foundation for today's popular songs. It links the music to the most common of human actions, from the human heartbeat to dance, work, and play. Pop rhythms have grown and developed over the years into a diverse collection of styles and approaches. On one end of the spectrum you find basic rock beats, anchored by simple bass drum downbeats, sparked by snare accents, and held in place by the hi-hat pulse. On the other end are highly developed funk and hip-hop rhythms, heavily syncopated and colored by an array of special effects, electronic sounds, loops, and samples. The rhythms are different, yet they share certain common elements, all traceable to the original formulas from which the styles have grown. The rhythm approaches heard today on the radio and performed in many types of bands represent only the most recent stages of a series of evolutionary steps going back decades and even centuries.

For the new rhythm player who is on the cutting edge of developments in music and instrumentation and who is involved in creating drum beats for original music, it is helpful to go back and connect with the old—with the traditions that have laid the groundwork for current and future sounds. The cliché "there is nothing new under the sun" might raise the hackles of some artists who stand by the pure originality of their work, but in the final analysis, current music couldn't exist without the preparations of previous history and preceding music. Every new creation is in some way a synthesis of what has come before—a blending and intermingling of old ideas that, when approached from a new perspective and interpreted in a new voice, are broadened and turned into something fresh and original. This has certainly been true in the development of pop music, with interpretations of blues and country for example, yielding the hybrid form of rock and roll.

Rhythm itself, as used in the pop music we play and listen to today, is ultimately the result of two converging traditions: the European classical practices from which we also draw much of our harmony, melody, and sense of form and African folk idioms and ideas, which have brought to American music the vital elements of spontaneity and syncopated rhythmic freedom. Let's examine the two traditions separately and then look at how their convergence has shaped the diverse rhythms in current popular use.

## TRACING THE WESTERN TRADITION

Rhythm in the Western tradition ("Western" meaning essentially the European classical forms) has not had a central role in the sense of prominent rhythm instruments used to set up a beat.

The concept of rhythm has instead been tied in closely with the idea of melodic motion, the duration of notes, and the rate and flow of their movement. Therefore to discuss rhythm in this tradition, we also have to discuss melody

Prior to the twelfth century, the primary form of music in the Western classical tradition was apparently monophonic, or music consisting of a single melodic line without additional harmony or accompaniment. It is generally referred to as "plainsong," and is the style both of Greek music and Gregorian chant. The music probably stretched from nonrhythmical to rhythmically regular and from nonmelodic and monotonous to quite complex. Gregorian chant is generally conceded to have had considerable rhythmic freedom, though scholars still debate the exact rhythmic nature of most early forms of music. It was with the rise of polyphony and more elaborate musical forms that we can really begin to trace rhythm through history to the present.

Polyphony means "many sounds" and refers to the simultaneous use of two or more melodic lines, each with individual significance and independence. Polyphony didn't really begin to develop until the middle of the twelfth century though there were some indications of earlier uses. The first proliferation of measured rhythm occurred from 1150 to 1250, with the use of *rhythmic modes*. These modes developed into the system called *mensural rhythm*, which was the precursor of the modern system.

Early polyphony required rhythmical organization, and the rhythmic modes set up a very basic system. The modes consisted of short rhythmic phrases that were combined to create extended rhythms. They were made up of combinations of two lengths of tones, long and short. These rhythmic patterns were used more or less consistently in polyphonic composition, with each individual part adhering to one mode. Two simple melodies with simple, repeating rhythms were played independently or, as we would say today, in counterpoint.

During this period, units of three were considered to be perfect time and all of the modes were grouped in time measures of three beats. Triple time dominated the musical world, though duple time was also in occasional use. Written in modern notation, the rhythms that created the six commonly known rhythm modes of this time are shown below:

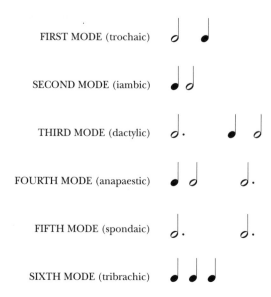

During much of the polyphonic period, 1260 to 1600, a different and more complete system of duple and triple meter came into use, called mensural rhythm (meaning "measured rhythm"). This system was necessitated by growth in rhythmic complexity and greater use of duple meter.

Mensural rhythm differed in notation from the modern form in that it contained no bar lines, no ties, and no triplets. Rather than using triplets, it used perfect and imperfect forms of notes, a holdover from the modes. Below are shown the original forms of mensural rhythm:

*The Rhythm Book*

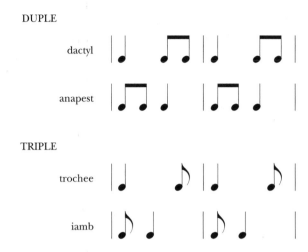

Theoretically, mensural rhythm is meter without stress, as heard in the almost stressless flow of Renaissance polyphony. Subsequent mensural rhythms, however, required accents, as in the meters below:

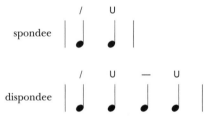

Eventually, meter and time signature became linked, and meter became an underlying rhythm rather than the actual played or sung rhythm.

Eventually, meter and time signature became linked, and meter became an underlying rhythm rather than the actual played or sung rhythm.

The Baroque period, 1600 to 1750, saw a shift from polyphonic to homophonic music and from mensural rhythm to the modern system. The advent of monody, music for a single singer with accompaniment, marked this turning point. As polyphonic music was abandoned and accompanied melody was introduced, rhythms became subordinate to melody. The simple and strong body rhythms of the Baroque period were indicative of the association of most of this music with dance, just as today's pop music is closely associated with dance.

Homophonic music, referring to a single melody line supported by chords or other subordinate material, has been the dominant form in Western music from 1600 to the present (though there has been a renewed interest in polyphony in this century). Homophonic music generally makes less of a demand on the listener than does polyphony. With the development of homophonic music, rhythm evolved into the modern metrical system, based on time signature and meter rather than on repeating rhythms previously called meters.

The Rococo period, from 1710 to 1775, emphasized pleasantness and prettiness in a similar fashion to the art of the day and in contrast to the seriousness and dignity of Baroque. In general, the newfound use of harmony in seventeenth and eighteenth century music tended to limit rhythmic subtleties and flexibility in the use of stress accents. While conforming to our modern notions of meter, music of this period was rhythmically very simple.

The same was true of the Classical period, roughly bounded by the years 1750 to 1820. Although marked by great and enduring pieces of music, the Classical period retained most of the rhythmic simplicity and metric constraints of the earlier styles.

The Romantic period occupied most of the nineteenth century, and, while progressing through several stages, extended the freedom of rhythm and meter within attempts to achieve powerfully emotional expression. A significant rhythmic development was the use of syncopation, beginning in the late works of Beethoven. While syncopation was found in some fourteenth century French music, it was largely absent from the Western tradition until the Romantic period. Syncopation and other advanced rhythmic concepts didn't occupy a central place in Western music until music from other cultures—notably Africa—began to exert a stronger influence in the West.

An interesting aspect of the development of music during this period is the change that occurred in musical practice after around 1850. Up until that time, musicians were naturally composers and improvisers as well as interpreters of other people's music. Keyboard players would improvise accompaniments based on written numbers called *figured bass*. After 1850, composing became a specialized skill. The ability of classical musicians to learn by ear and to improvise has greatly diminished since that time. In popular music, the ability to play by ear, improvise, and compose may be more integrally combined, as they were prior to 1850. Some contemporary classical musicians have looked to popular music as a means of rediscovering and developing these essential musical skills.

In the twentieth century, there has been a tremendous acceleration in the development of rhythm in Western music. Much of this development, beginning with the primitivistic rhythms of early twentieth century composers, has come from cross-cultural and popular forms of music. In general, the line between popular and classical forms has blurred, and many amalgamations of musical styles have appeared within various contexts. Lively Slavic dance rhythms and the complex syncopations of jazz have been very influential in much of contemporary music. Within jazz itself, where rhythmic syncopation is often referred to as the hallmark of the musical form, rhythms and rhythmic formats have developed greatly

Though classical music has borrowed heavily from popular and non-Western forms, its own profound impact can be measured in terms of the most basic, widely accepted concepts such as the homophonic structure of music (simple melody with harmony). It has also produced pioneers in the field of electronic music and new technology. The use of electronic instruments, computers, and nonmusical sounds—an active part of contemporary music-making—were first explored by classical composers like Pierre Boulez, Karlheinz Stockhausen, and John Cage.

# CHAPTER 6

# The African Connection

Perhaps the most fascinating aspect of rhythm's evolution has been the introduction of African-derived approaches into the Western tradition.

Perhaps the most fascinating aspect of rhythm's evolution has been the introduction of African-derived approaches into the Western tradition. We can hear it in modern dance music from Madonna to Dr. Dre, in jazz and blues, and in rock and roll. The African influence is present in nearly every phase of pop music: the improvisation of vocalists, jazz musicians, rock guitarists, and all kinds of drummers; the "call and response" structure of back-up singers echoing lead vocalists and snare backbeats answering bass drum pulses; the "blue notes" that are the melodic centerpieces of rock and jazz; the syncopation that lifts standard four-four rhythm to more catchy levels of tension and interest; the inflection and voice-like sounds of instruments, including some of the electronic drums in current use; and the "swing" feel of accenting and shifting beats, of stating musical ideas obliquely and indirectly rather than directly and on-the-beat. These elements are such an intrinsic part of the way we hear and play music that we're often not aware of them at all.

Before tracing the flow of African rhythm into the vast mainstream of American pop, it's valuable to examine the significant features of the African tradition before it interacted with the West.

## THE AFRICAN TRADITION

In the music of Africa, the drum is as central an element as the piano and violin are in the Western classical tradition. Rhythm plays the primary musical role, just as melody does in European practice.

In the music of Africa, the drum is as central an element as the piano and violin are in the Western classical tradition. Rhythm plays the primary musical role, just as melody does in European practice.

The drum—as the central tool—is augmented with batteries of all kinds of percussion instruments. (African drums and percussion instruments are cousins of the Latin-American percussion instruments described in the last chapter.) The talking drum, as shown here, vital in traditional West African forms and still used prominently in popular cross-cultural African bands, is one of the few instruments from the African arsenal that did not later take root in Latin and South America.

*Modern talking drum*

The talking drum appears in a variety of sizes and shapes. The pitch of the drum is stretched up by pulling the cord (or a handle in modern versions) attached to the center of the drum head. Through intricate interactions between striking and stretching the head, the player can produce remarkable voice-like sounds, inflections, and melodies. The infinitely flexible sound of the talking drum places it at the opposite end of the spectrum from many synthesizer based drum sounds, with their essentially synthetic, rigid timbres. It embodies the element of "feel" in rhythm.

**In the African tradition, playing an instrument is an extension of singing —bringing vocal nuance, inflection, and ambiguity of tone to all instruments.**

The vocal quality of this instrument points to the purpose and use of rhythm in African society. Folk music expresses unspoken versions of stories, proverbs, and legends. The drums tell the stories, with specific rhythms communicating different parts of the narrative. Music is also a central part of formal and informal functions and is used to announce births and deaths, mark arrivals and departures (especially for hunting), find lost children, and teach the young about the environment. In the African tradition, playing an instrument is an extension of singing —bringing vocal nuance, inflection, and ambiguity of tone to all instruments.

Rhythm and inflection are, in many ways, the strongest distinguishing elements of African music. Both elements may be applied broadly, with rhythmic complexity evident in melody as well as accompaniment, and inflection relating to both rhythmic and tonal aspects of music.

Traditional African melody employs dissonance and tones of indeterminate pitch. The dissonance occurs in the combination of melodic parts, as there is no harmony in the Western chordal sense. The secondary melodies—or counter-melodies to the main theme—often take the form of repeated short motifs that are sung or played, similar to what is sometimes called a riff in blues or jazz. The dissonance frequently takes the form of the *blue notes* of jazz—the flatted third, fifth, and seventh.

Another prominent part of African melody is antiphony (from the Greek *antiphonia* or "counter sound"). Antiphony refers to the call and response vocal format in which a phrase is sung and followed by an answer phrase. The call and response may be carried out by a soloist and a chorus or by two choruses. The phrases may overlap and become quite elaborate.

A key element of music in Africa, and one that is also found in early Western traditions, is improvisation. African music is improvisational on all levels of rhythm and melody within a complex and rigorous discipline, whether sung or played on an instrument.

These basic elements of the African tradition have had an enormous impact on popular music in the West, although in their integrated form they are far different from the way they were in their original setting. Whole aspects of African music, such as the folklore forms that communicate elaborate messages through specific rhythms, have not been absorbed into Western music. Our examination of these concepts will focus on their current structure and makeup as they have become used in the West, not as they exist in traditional African music. But before looking at and learning to play some of these borrowed rhythmic elements, let's follow the flow of African music to the West and into the familiar styles that we've been playing and listening to for decades.

The slave trade from Africa to the West in the eighteenth and nineteenth centuries brought certain cultural gifts along with its legacy of suffering and injustice. It is a testament to the strength and vitality of African music and culture that, in spite of its being uprooted, transplanted, and suppressed, many of its basic elements were able to survive and flourish in a new and foreign setting.

The slaves came primarily from the western coast of Africa, though they were also brought from central, southern, and eastern sections. Under English and American subjugation they were taken to the islands of the Caribbean and to the east coast of North America. Under the Portuguese and the Spanish they were sent to Brazil and Venezuela. Though slave customs differed greatly in these far-flung settings, there remain striking similarities in the survival of the musical culture.

In Latin America and the Caribbean, the music of the displaced Africans was allowed free expression. African traditions took hold and began exerting widespread influence in popular and dance music. They are most clearly identifiable in the music of Haiti, which exhibits a direct link to African sources, and in the Afro-Cuban tradition through its extraordinarily complex rhythm patterns and instrumental timbres used in song and dance accompaniment.

In contrast to the ease with which African influence blended with Latin-American practices, those same influences were slow to come into North American popular music. Part of the reason was that slaves were commonly prohibited from dancing, drumming, and pursuing other forms of musical expression. In Joseph Conrad's *Heart of Darkness*, the drums beat when "the natives were restless," and in the United States drumming came to symbolize the culture that the white man intended to eradicate in the name of enlightened progress. (Drumming, of course, had been integrated into all aspects of African cultures and represented far more than expressions of aggression.) Still, African music managed to develop in various locations in the American South, and ultimately followed a circuitous—though not well documented—route into American music.

Among the musical forms that grew out of the Southern fields and plantations were spirituals, West African work songs, and field hollers. The latter two are cited as being precursors to country-blues, which, along with black religious music, became a root form of American pop. Each of these combined African concepts with elements drawn from the European harmonic tradition. The black spiritual, which borrowed harmony from English Protestant hymns, also rested on a call and response relationship between the vocal soloist and an answering chorus, as well as African approaches to syncopation and vocal timbre. The blues, while resting firmly on a European I-IV-V chord structure, also exhibited a call and response form in the tendency of vocal lines to be answered by guitar lines. Both spirituals and blues employed the African-based element of improvisation.

The "Negro marching bands" employed improvisation, call and response, and other musical practices brought from Africa, which, though foreign to most of the listeners, were mixed with sufficiently traditional elements to be widely accepted.

Although the specific locations of pop music origin are open to debate, New Orleans proved to be a seeding ground of particular importance, especially with regard to the birth of the popular instrumental tradition. At the start of the nineteenth century, New Orleans was evenly divided between the French and the Spanish on the one hand, and the Africans on the other. The lines of demarcation between the two cultures were not rigidly drawn. Both Catholicism and Vodun, a religion derived from African ancestor worship, were practiced by all races. The overall outlook was permissive, due to the melting pot nature of the New Orleans population and the city's role as a prosperous port and a center of trade. The drum was never banned in Louisiana, nor was dancing prohibited.

The intermingling of races, culture, and musical traditions made New Orleans a prime site for the early growth of jazz. A movement of consequence in jazz development, linked to the city's affinity for all things French, was its enthusiastic adoption of Napoleon's favored ensemble, the military band. The "Negro marching bands" that evolved from the concept of the military band were first used to provide music at funerals. By the mid-nineteenth century, they were so popular that they were hired for all kinds of functions by all segments of New Orleans society. These bands employed improvisation, call and response, and other musical practices brought from Africa, which, though foreign to most of the listeners, were mixed with sufficiently traditional elements to be widely accepted.

Smaller combinations of these brass bands began to play for dancers in places of entertainment in New Orleans. It was in Storyville, the famed red light district in the turn-of-the-century French Quarter, that the jazz pianist came into being, playing in a style that was later to be called boogie-woogie. An early form of syncopated music called ragtime developed, and the accompanying dance, the cakewalk, created a controversial sensation. (Although ragtime was hailed by some as America's new music, it was also condemned as vulgar, suggestive, and un-American.) Along with syncopated rhythms, ragtime used European harmonies and elements of the John Philip Sousa marches that were the most popular music of the day. When Storyville was closed down in 1917, many of the unemployed jazzmen traveled up the Mississippi to Kansas City and Chicago, both of which became centers of jazz and blues.

The country-blues style, consisting of solo vocalist with acoustic guitar accompaniment, spread from its Southern origins in the early twentieth century and provided the foundation for later classic blues performances of singers backed by full bands. Recordings by popular vocalists such as Ma Rainey and Bessie Smith brought national recognition to the music in the twenties.

In the Northern cities, the blues later began to take an electric slant, combining amplified guitars and harmonies with keyboard, bass, and drums. Urban blues bands proliferated during the thirties and forties, yielding a number of national hits.

**...all of these styles retained the shouting vocal inflection, syncopated rhythm, call-and-response voice/instrument patterns, and improvisation that stemmed from African culture's entry into the West.**

A further development of the blues, called rhythm and blues, blended gospel/shout vocals with blues harmonies and rhythms drawn from swing and boogie-woogie. Originally promulgated in the late thirties and forties by jump bands like Louis Jordan's Tympany Five and the Harlem Hamfats, rhythm and blues eventually laid the groundwork for rock and roll under the high-energy stylings of Little Richard and Fats Domino. Elvis Presley blended it with country sounds in the mid-fifties, yielding an early rock and roll precursor called rockabilly. And all of these styles retained the shouting vocal inflection, syncopated rhythm, call-and-response voice/instrument patterns, and improvisation that stemmed from African culture's entry into the West.

In the sixties R&B split off into two directions. The first was soul music, heavily dependent on the smooth vocal approach of former gospel singers like Sam Cooke and Clyde McPhatter. As the style grew in popularity along with artists like Marvin Gaye, Stevie Wonder, The Temptations, The Supremes, Otis Redding, and Aretha Franklin, the rhythms grew more refined, streamlining the rough-hewn swing/shuffle/boogie-woogie beats of earlier days into smooth, propulsive, pop underpinnings. The second offshoot was funk, a flashier, more exciting form that evolved from the stop-on-a-dime precision of James Brown's band through the gospel/rock/ funk/psychedelic anthems of Sly and the Family Stone. Both styles metamorphosed in the seventies: soul into the rhythmically homogeneous, studio slick disco; funk into more of the funky same—aided, abetted, and refined by the addition of synthesized percussion and new slap bass techniques.

White rock musicians drew from the blues/R&B tradition as well. Much of the Beatles' early popularity stemmed from their regurgitation of Little Richard tunes and black U.S. rhythms, while the Stones enjoyed similar success by borrowing from Chuck Berry and other blues-based artists. In the late sixties, a number of white players and bands locked on to Chicago blues and hammered it into a fiery virtuosic form that paved the way for hard rock and heavy metal. Among these artists were Eric Clapton, Jimmy Page, Jeff Beck, Fleetwood Mac, and Canned Heat.

Jazz, meanwhile, had undergone another set of changes subsequent to the early days of ragtime, boogie-woogie, and brass bands. As the music spread to various urban centers in the first part of this century, the styles expanded, blended in with other approaches, and coalesced into new forms. Among them was swing music. Though swing is broadly defined as an approach to performance encompassing particular rhythmic variations, it also refers to the style of jazz that dominated the thirties, played by numerous big bands and small groups. The time shifting aspect of swing was further refined in the forties with the clamorous arrival of bebop. Kenny Clarke, Max Roach, Elvin Jones, and other drummers in this style stretched out the syncopation factor until an entirely new rhythm was implied, drawing jazz drumming ever closer to polyrhythm. The impact of swing and bebop drumming has stayed with jazz ever since, providing the model approach from which further explorations into syncopation, polyrhythm, and free rhythm have been launched.

Fueled by the combined force of these stylistic elements, current pop music (jazz inclusive) continues to expand and develop while maintaining fully integrated and refined versions of well-established rhythmic/harmonic concepts. The traditions that are at the root of today's forms and approaches were virtually unknown in the West prior to the turn of the century.

Again, it is a tribute to the strength of these African-based musical concepts that they have exerted such an important influence in such a relatively short period of time. Some of them are now absolutely central to virtually all styles of popular music. Let's take a closer look at those concepts that are most important to pop rhythm.

## SYNCOPATION AND THE BACKBEAT

The widespread use of syncopation in popular music today is primarily the result of influences from other cultures, especially African. As defined in Chapter 3, syncopation is any abnormality in meter, such as an accented beat on a normally unaccented beat. By extending syncopation throughout a piece of music, one can effectively create a new meter, or a new underlying sense of accentuation. It is a form of abnormal meter, or syncopation, that yields one of the cornerstones of pop music: the backbeat.

The now immortalized "backbeat, you can't lose it"—also called "fatback"—has provided current music with a catchy offbeat hook and has brought about an essential shift in the way rhythm feels.

Listen to almost any pop song and you'll hear it. The now immortalized "backbeat, you can't lose it"—also called "fatback"—has provided current music with a catchy offbeat hook and has brought about an essential shift in the way rhythm feels. In the Western classical tradition, rhythm is smooth and flowing, in support of melody and harmony. In music with a backbeat, rhythm adopts a new internal logic; it has a built-in tension, a constantly recurring suspension and release. The use of the backbeat has changed the way we respond to rhythm while increasing the overall importance of rhythmic feel to the music.

The backbeat refers to accents placed on beats 2 and 4, answering "back" to the normally accented beats 1 and 3 in $\frac{4}{4}$ meter. The backbeats may be obviously stated, as they usually are in popular music, or they may be subtly felt, as is more common in traditional African music. In either case, they do not supersede beats 1 and 3 but interact with them to create an internal form of call and response. The measure is rhythmically centered on beat 1 (the primary resolution); by accenting beat 2, we provide an answer or response to the feeling of arrival on beat 1. This action is repeated with beat 3 (the secondary resolution) and the beat 4 response. Examine the following diagram and compare it to the traditional $\frac{4}{4}$ meter shown on page 22.

In most popular music, this relationship is expressed by bass drum hits on beats 1 and 3, answered by the snare drum on 2 and 4.

To focus on the difference in feel between the backbeat rhythm and the traditional Western approach, consider the following question: If an audience is clapping along with a song, which beats do they clap on?

To focus on the difference in feel between the backbeat rhythm and the traditional Western approach, consider the following question: If an audience is clapping along with a song, which beats do they clap on? A classically trained audience, or one that is unfamiliar with rock and pop rhythm, is likely to clap on beats 1 and 3 (even though the band and the snare drum are pushing the backbeat). A typical jazz or gospel audience will clap on beats 2 and 4, feeling these accents as an essential response to beats 1 and 3. Even though the backbeat is completely integrated into popular music—the audience and even the musicians may not have fully integrated it into the way they feel the pulse. Experiment with clapping or tapping your foot along with music that you're familiar with. Try clapping on all four beats, then just on beats 1 and 3, then try clapping only on beats 2 and 4 (the backbeat). When clapping on the backbeat, we still feel 1 and 3 as strong beats, with the backbeat providing a response to them. This adds up to a much more involved approach to pulse-keeping than is employed in traditional music—the backbeat is already featured prominently in popular music, yet our response to it and feel for it will vary.

Accentuation, whether applied to the backbeat or to other beats, has been used widely in popular music. The importance of accenting in determining sound quality and the way its use differs in pop and classical music is illustrated in a basic saxophone technique. In blues-based music, sax players tend to tongue every note (use their tongue on the reed at the start of the note to produce a strong attack). In classical music, the sax player plays most notes legato (flowing from one note to the other without attacking each one). The sax player who tongues every note has the ability to provide varying degrees of accent to most of the notes played. He is using accent and inflection to enhance the vocal quality of his instrument. The following examples apply accenting to simply rhythms to produce syncopation. The > indicates an accented note. Notice that these rhythms all include the backbeat accents, and the last two rhythms are further syncopated in their omission of beat 3.

Although swing has been used to define a particular style of jazz, it refers most often to an approach to playing in which the placement of notes is shifted slightly in relationship to the beat.

More systematic manipulations of accent and inflection led to the concept of swing."Although swing has been used to define a particular style of jazz, it refers most often to an approach to playing in which the placement of notes is shifted slightly in relationship to the beat. This is often described as playing "in front of the beat" or "behind the beat." Put differently, the attack of a given note may be placed slightly before or after the mathematically proper place relative to the pulse, yielding a looser, more syncopated feeling. A consistent pattern of this kind of manipulation is a prominent feature of jazz, and it makes it nearly impossible to notate the music exactly as it should be played. For this reason, the swing factor in a given piece of written music is often indicated by a verbal instruction at the top of the score. New technology as discussed later in this book, has made it much easier to record and analyze the subtle nuances of the swing feel.

## POLYRHYTHM

Polyrhythm, like syncopation, is a broad musical concept that may be applied in numerous ways. In the most general sense, polyrhythm is the simultaneous use of rhythms that do not agree in subdivision and or meter. As you will see, this may take a variety of forms which vary in use and complexity.

Polyrhythm, in its simplest form, may be described as an extension of syncopation and phrasing. If we extend some of the basic concepts of syncopation that were shown in Chapter 3 we may produce a very simple polyrhythm. By playing consistently on the off beat (the "and" beats that divide the primary beats), we briefly establish the feeling of a new pulse, offset from the underlying beat. This new pulse suggests an alternative beat, disconnected from, though related to, the primary beat. As discussed previously, this may be called a cross-pulse.

**P** = primary beat (in this example sounded only on the 1 beat of the first measure)
**A** = alternate beat (in this example sounded in between each primary beat)

We can also create a polyrhythm by using rhythmic phrases made up of note groups other than the usual numerical divisions of the time signature. In the following one-bar examples, the rhythm is phrased in three-beat groups. The effect is that of superimposing a three-beat cycle over a two-beat pulse. The rhythm has two groups of three and then a final group of two, completing the eight-beat cycle of the measure. Count this rhythm in four with accents, then try counting it as two groups of three and a group of two. The curved lines indicate the natural phrasing.

**What is the difference between two against three and three against two?**

Sometimes a polyrhythmic effect is created by the interaction of many syncopated lines, even though no obvious counter-phrase, such as the one above, is used. The overall effect is of many rhythms and phrases suggesting all kinds of contrary beat groups and meters. This is especially common in jazz and in other improvised settings.

Another kind of polyrhythm expands on the simple use of phrasing to produce cross-pulses. The two most common kinds of cross-pulses, two against three and three against two, are called hemiola. Hemiola is the term for note values standing in relationship of three to two. What is the difference between two against three and three against two? The ultimate effect is similar; the difference lies in getting there. Both of these rhythms are implied in two basic components of the notational system: the dotted note and the triplet. As you shall see, the dotted note arrives at hemiola by superimposing a 2-pulse over a previously established 3; the triplet fits a 3-pulse over a preset 2. Let's explore this further.

We'll begin in $\frac{3}{4}$ time. The beat is a quarter note, grouped into threes by bar lines. You emphasize the feeling of three by accenting each 1 beat in keeping with standard $\frac{3}{4}$ meter. Before going on, remember that a dotted note is equal to the value of the note plus one-half the value of the note (one dotted quarter note = one-and-a-half quarter notes). Clearly then, two dotted quarter notes are equal in value to three quarter notes. By playing a series of dotted quarter notes against a quarter note pulse in $\frac{3}{4}$ time, you produce the effect of a 2-pulse combined with a 3-pulse. Hemiola is created by a movement from a three pulse, to a relationship of two to three, as shown below.

The same effect may be created by moving in the opposite direction. Here we begin in $\frac{4}{4}$ time. We now have a quarter-note beat that, as defined by the meter, is felt in groups of two. Our definition of a triplet—three notes played in place of two notes of the same value—serves to create hemiola. The top example below shows how we would move from a two pulse to a relationship of three to two by using a quarter-note triplet. In the second example, we break the quarter note triplets into two groups of eighth-note triplets to get a different perspective on this rhythm. By creating six triplet notes we can more clearly see the relationship of the 2-pulse (understood as two groups of three) to the 3-pulse (breaking up the same six notes into three groups of two). The eighth-note triplet is a common subdivision in jazz and hemiola of this type.

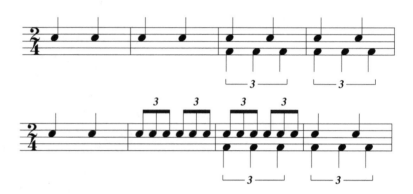

Using either of these techniques yields the same ultimate effect of hemiola. By reversing the direction of movement, however, one creates a very different underlying feeling of pulse.

It may be very difficult to execute these rhythms and especially to produce smooth sounding transitions and even sounding pulses. If you have access to a sequencer, program these rhythms—listen, and clap or play along until it becomes comfortable.

The above examples yield two-line rhythms, but we may also create hemiola as a one-line rhythm that maintains its polyrhythm in relation to the underlying (but not played) beat. The two examples below create identical rhythms, though each has a different basic meter. The first rhythm is in $\frac{3}{4}$ and the underlying pulse is felt as groups of three. The second rhythm, in $\frac{2}{4}$, is felt as groups of two. Both rhythms move back and forth between pulses in two and pulses in three; the difference is in the underlying feeling (which should be maintained by tapping the foot on the quarter-note beat). It may be very difficult to execute these rhythms and especially to produce smooth sounding transitions and even sounding pulses. If you have access to a sequencer, program these rhythms—listen, and clap or play along until it becomes comfortable. You have only really mastered hemiola when you can play these rhythms quite comfortably feeling either pulse (the two or the three) and maintaining either beat in the tapping of your foot.

Another way of arriving at hemiola is through changing time signatures, also called polymeter. In the next example, $\frac{3}{4}$ time signature shifts to $\frac{6}{8}$. Meter defines the $\frac{3}{4}$ time signature (played in eighth notes) as having a feeling of three groups of two beats each, whereas $\frac{6}{8}$ time is felt as two groups of three beats each. In the example, the rhythm that is clapped (a simple eighth-note pulse) remains constant while the beat (tapped by the foot) goes from groups of three in $\frac{3}{4}$ to groups of two in $\frac{6}{8}$. The value of the eighth note remains the same, so the pulse that is clapped keeps the same speed throughout. The beat shifts when the signature changes, so that the tapping foot changes from three to a bar to two to a bar. The underlying feeling (meter) is creating a form of hemiola. This may also be difficult to coordinate, so begin by using a very slow tempo.

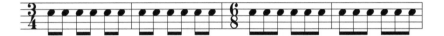

Further polyrhythmic effects can be created by mixing a variety of rhythms with the use of changing time signatures.

The concept of polymeter suggests an element of African rhythm that has only found limited application in the West: the additive approach. In general, rhythm can be created either by dividing the pulse into varying note lengths or by adding new rhythms without regard to previous note groupings. These techniques may be called *divisive* and *additive*, respectively. The two methods represent very different ways of feeling the creation of rhythm, though they may yield rhythms that sound the same. The Western system of meter and time signature is linked with the divisive approach; the underlying pulse is divided up into measures and varying note values. In an additive approach, rhythmic phrases are added together, one after another, to produce a string of rhythm. Polymeter reflects this in its creation of phrases that may or may not contain the same number of beats. The divisive method may offer a nice, consistent system for producing rhythm, but the additive approach may be more natural.

...rhythm can be created either by dividing the pulse into varying note lengths or by adding new rhythms without regard to previous note groupings.

**Sequencers give us ready access to all kinds of polyrhythmic effects that would otherwise take years to master or would be virtually impossible to reproduce.**

Polyrhythm may extend beyond any of the notions we've described so far. An extreme form of polyrhythm is free rhythm, employing many simultaneous independent rhythmic lines. The pulses and phrases of the lines may not share any common elements of the beat, although they usually maintain separate internal structures in the form of pulse and phrase. Free rhythm of this type has been used in various forms of jazz and by certain twentieth century classical composers. The effect may range from a feeling of suspension to cacophonous to simply unmusical. The listener's perception, however, is probably conditioned by his or her musical background and experience. What is meaningless noise to one listener may be entirely musical to another.

Sequencers give us ready access to all kinds of polyrhythmic effects that would otherwise take years to master or would be virtually impossible to reproduce.

Experiment with some of the examples here and work out your own extensions of polyrhythm. If you own a drum machine, you can do this fairly easily, and the rhythms may suggest some fresh ideas for your own drum parts and song structures.

# CHAPTER 7

# Popular Rhythm Traditions

Just as we use language by combining words to form phrases, phrases to make sentences, and sentences to make paragraphs, so do we build extended rhythms from notes to phrases and phrases to sections, with the measure serving to identify the basic structural units.

he blending of several rhythm traditions has resulted in the diversity of pop styles that make up today's musical landscape. It is to your advantage to know the fine points of rhythm in all these styles, so that you are able to apply them intelligently to whatever music you happen to be writing, arranging, producing, or setting to rhythm. Before looking at narrow divisions of rock, urban, country, and jazz, however, it will be helpful to look at the broader categories of music from which they have emerged.

There are two basic traditions which can be seen as "umbrella" styles for all of contemporary popular music. One of them is the pop tradition, which in its broadest definition can be said to embrace most categories of the contemporary popular song. The other is the jazz tradition, which in an equally broad definition might include a large majority of popular instrumental music. Within each of these categories are basic rhythms that can later be expanded and adjusted to fit various spin-off styles. The following discussion will focus on these essential rhythms, presenting them in a two-line format that you can practice using two hands in preparation for the more complex drum beats that will be presented in Part Three.

As you explore rhythms common to basic popular styles, it's also valuable to begin thinking about ways these rhythms are expanded into complete instrumental arrangements, with specific functions assigned to guitars, keyboards, bass guitars, and supplementary "sweetening" instruments. In this way, rhythm can be seen to encompass much more than drum and percussion parts. You might also start to consider the larger rhythmic issues of form, in which small segments of rhythm are linked together to create songs and complete compositions. Just as we use language by combining words to form phrases, phrases to make sentences, and sentences to make paragraphs, so do we build extended rhythms from notes to phrases and phrases to sections, with the measure serving to identify the basic structural units.

The influences on pop music have come from an even greater number of sources than we've previously seen. Among the other rhythm traditions that have been absorbed, in varying degrees, into the melting pot of mainstream pop are those of Latin America and the Far East. Though their impact has been limited, these traditions provide the contemporary drummer with extra spice for a well-balanced recipe of rhythm sounds and techniques.

## THE POP TRADITION

**What is rhythmically fundamental to this popular vocal music is the use of the backbeat.**

Since the sixties, the term *pop* has come to include a wide range of approaches to popular music. Much of what is also called rock, country, blues, R&B, rap, hip-hop, and even jazz has in recent years been included under the pop heading. There are also many branches within each of these headings, with new categories and genres emerging on a regular basis. What is rhythmically fundamental to this popular vocal music is the use of the backbeat.

Some simple backbeat rhythms are shown here. In pop, the simplest and most common rhythms consist of variations using eighth notes set in $\frac{4}{4}$ time. The backbeat—or beats 2 and 4—is usually played on the snare drum, with the bass drum hitting at least on beats 1 and 3. Other instruments may be added to provide support on beats 2 and 4.

Dividing backbeat rhythms into two-line rhythms allows us to isolate the backbeat from the bass drum part. Two-line rhythms suggest the use of contrasting pitches and timbres (tone colors) for the upper and lower beats. Though many percussion instruments are of indeterminate pitch (that is, they don't have a defined pitch in terms of a specific note), they still can differ in relative pitch and tone color, such as with two conga drums of differing sizes. Indeed, the two-line rhythms shown on the next page are as playable on hand drums, congas, or the piano as they are on a drum set. The examples are labeled as R = right hand (bass drum) and L = left hand (snare drum) because most drummers play the snare drum with the left hand. If applied to congas or to piano, however, the hands would normally be reversed—on the piano the left hand (bass notes) would play the bass drum pattern and the right hand would play the backbeat.

Adding sixteenth notes and letting the backbeat (left) hand participate further in the rhythm yields the "funkier" and freer kinds of beats shown here. These two-pitched rhythms interact to form one rhythm, with the distinguishing backbeat emphasized through accentuation. These examples may require quite a bit of practice to master.

A pop group builds on top of rhythms such as these, meaning that each instrument takes a part that fits into or supports the basic rhythm stated by the bass drum and snare. The key elements in many groups are drums, bass (bass guitar or keyboard bass), one or more rhythm instruments (guitars and/or keyboards), and singers or rappers. Additional instruments or samples are used as desired for melodic, harmonic, and rhythmic support. The rhythmic hierarchy starts with the drums and progresses through bass, rhythm instruments, and melody. The drums provide the essential rhythms, including the pulse and backbeat; the bass bridges the drums to the harmony; and the rhythm instruments augment the rhythm and provide harmonic support for the melody. Let's look at the rhythmic role of each instrument.

**The only real rule of thumb here is that the bass and the bass drum, sharing the low register, will work together rhythmically in some fundamental way.**

The bass generally plays linear (single note) parts that are closely related to the drum rhythms but also provide fundamental harmonic information for the other instruments and singers. In many cases, the bass plays a simple pulse (usually eighth or quarter notes). If adopting a more rhythmic role, it may play the identical rhythm as the bass drum. This might involve covering the bass drum part while adding other rhythms, or it could be limited to playing a portion of the bass drum beat. Bass lines are often ostinato parts (repeating, as with a riff). The only real rule of thumb here is that the bass and the bass drum, sharing the low register, will work together rhythmically in some fundamental way. Any of the right-hand rhythms above (representing the bass drum) can be used as bass line rhythms.

The guitars and keyboards (now able to simulate virtually any instrumental sound) are usually the bridge linking the drums and bass to the vocal or melody. These rhythm instruments serve two basic functions. The first is to provide rhythmic support and contrast, and the second is to lay down a harmonic foundation. Usually both functions are fulfilled simultaneously by one instrument, though focusing on one or the other of the two tasks suggests some interesting arrangement possibilities.

In adopting a mostly rhythmic role, the instrument is usually played staccato (a very short-sounding note or chord) and is rhythmically active. Sixteenth-note rhythms are common to this approach, as is a pronounced attack. Although harmonic information is being presented, it is not making a very strong statement. The sound of the instrument is sometimes so short and played with such attack as to be essentially nonharmonic, producing a percussive sound almost like a scratch. Guitars and many keyboard sounds have very strong percussive capabilities and may be used strictly for rhythm.

The rhythm instrument may instead offer harmonic information with very little rhythmic content. These instrumental parts are sometimes called *pads* because they pad the overall sound with chordal harmony. A classic example of a pad is the organ part in the classic Percy Sledge song "When a Man Loves a Woman." In earlier popular song forms, the harmonic information was most often played on electronic organ or strings. Now these sustained harmonic backdrops can be assigned virtually any sound quality by using a synthesizer or a sampler.

**The most common style of rhythm playing on guitar or keyboard manages to combine these two functions, using sharp attack and well-placed sustain to both reinforce the rhythm and provide the harmony.**

The most common style of rhythm playing on guitar or keyboard manages to combine these two functions, using sharp attack and well-placed sustain to both reinforce the rhythm and provide the harmony. The rhythms are often built from the bass drum and bass parts, offering simple, basic outlines of the more complex drum/bass combination. The harmonic aspect of this approach supports the vocal line by including melody notes, often as the top note of the chord.

Background vocals, horn sections, percussion, and other instruments may be used to add further levels of rhythmic and harmonic information. At the top of the rhythmic hierarchy are solo vocal and instrumental melodies (lead vocal, lead guitar, and so on). Melodies tend to have the greatest rhythmic freedom, relying on the other instruments to provide the underlying support.

> Although phrases in popular songs tend to be very simple, with obvious signposts such as accented downbeats and resolutions to the primary chord, the instrumental phrase can be more mysterious and hard to define. Programming sequencers to create song forms can help you to structure interesting rhythmic phrases.

Rhythmic arranging requires attention to two basic types of organization: vertical and horizontal. Vertical arranging relates to the interaction of all instruments at any given moment. It tells you where the instruments coincide rhythmically and what the cumulative rhythmic effect is when they don't. The arranger who is focusing on vertical structure is concerned with the placement of the guitar relative to the hi-hat, using a bass note to fill a space left by the snare, finding a shaker part that will offer rhythmic counterpoint to the melody. In short, the vertical arranger is concerned with the instrumental groove that will be used throughout the song and that will provide an appropriate backdrop for the vocal.

Horizontal arranging refers to the order and interaction of the sections of a song. It describes the movement from part to part, such as the flow from introduction to verse to chorus, and so on. Horizontal arranging is necessarily defined in rhythmic terms, with the measure serving as the central unit of measurement. Rhythmic ideas tend to be in two and four measure phrases, which are developed into song sections that are usually eight, twelve, or sixteen measures long. The exact makeup of a phrase is dependent on the subtle interaction of all musical elements and rests in part on the perception of the listener. Although phrases in popular songs tend to be very simple, with obvious signposts such as accented downbeats and resolutions to the primary chord, the instrumental phrase can be more mysterious and hard to define. Programming sequencers to create song forms can help you to structure interesting rhythmic phrases.

## THE JAZZ TRADITION

The contemporary instrumental music tradition may be generally placed under the heading of jazz. In this sense, jazz could include music also called rock, blues, funk, fusion, new age, and even country (David Grisman's mandolin-based instrumental music, for example, is a rare mixing of jazz with bluegrass). At the core of the jazz tradition, however, is a rhythm that is also used widely in the blues: the shuffle or swing beat. It is to this basic concept that we will limit the present discussion, though you should keep in mind that these rhythms are expanded and developed to a great degree in the real world of instrumental music, as well as in Part Three of this book.

*The Rhythm Book*

At the core of the jazz tradition is a rhythm that is also used widely in the blues: the shuffle or swing beat.

Shuffle and swing rhythms share a characteristic division of the beat by triplets rather than by straight eighth notes. Triplet rhythms are generally more complex than eighth-note rhythms because they suggest twelve divisions in a standard measure of $\frac{4}{4}$, rather than eight. As in pop, the backbeat is often played by the snare drum. The basic two-line rhythms shown below are written for two hands, which correspond to typical bass drum and snare drum patterns.

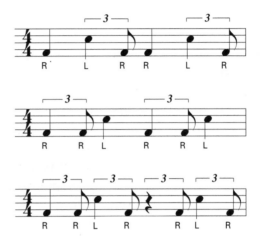

These rhythms are quite simple, employing only the first and third notes within each triplet. The following two-line rhythms suggest triplet ideas that are more developed. The backbeat may or may not be overtly stated, but it is implied in the underlying meter. Notice that the third one of these rhythms includes an example of hemiola (a simultaneous subdivision of the beat by two and three). This is a somewhat natural occurrence when using a three-note subdivision because groups of six may be organized as two groups of three, or three groups of two.

The rhythmic relationship of instruments in a typical jazz group is not unlike that in a pop band. The hierarchy still progresses from drums to bass, then to rhythm instruments, and finally to melody. The difference is that in a jazz unit the instruments often interact with more freedom and complexity than they might in a song-oriented setting.

**While the jazz tradition has expanded in many different directions, two important elements have remained relatively constant: syncopation and improvisation.**

While the jazz tradition has expanded in many different directions, two important elements have remained relatively constant: syncopation and improvisation. Both have occurred in simple and more complex forms. In early jazz groups, including the big bands of the swing era, syncopation was expressed in straightforward, off-the-beat accents by the horn section, the percussive accompaniment of the piano, and the single note lines of the soloist. Charlie Christian's guitar solos often made use of plainly stated, easy-to-follow syncopation. Many jazz soloists have played in straight eighth notes while syncopating the interior accents, as in the following:

In later small group approaches, evolving from the bebop groups of the forties, the syncopation factor began to be expanded throughout the ensemble, yielding even more complex offbeats that eventually spilled over into polyrhythm.

Improvisation in early jazz was carried out by the soloist, while the backup musicians provided solid and predictable support. Later groups turned improvisation into a complex, interactive form, in which each musician creates spontaneously while leading, answering, and always listening to the collaborating players.

In most jazz, the complexities of syncopation and improvisation occur within a broad structural framework. This framework may be borrowed directly from a song. In fact, many jazz compositions are arrangements of popular songs, using the original melody and chord structure as a jump-off point for improvisation. The traditional jazz format consists of a statement of the melody (the head), followed by a series of

> Though technology holds the promise of machine-generated improvisation and has delivered some composing software already, true improvisation is sure to remain a uniquely human capability.

improvisations based on the melody and ending with a restatement of the melody. Rhythmic frameworks—the horizontal arrangement cited earlier—may take a number of forms, from the twelve bar blues to the standard thirty-two bar song form (four eight-bar sections often organized as AABA) to the more contemporary verse/chorus format to the freer arrangements of some current ensembles.

Within these broad formats, jazz employs several rhythmic concepts that challenge the player and the listener. Among them are additive rhythms that are polyrhythmic and polymetric, yielding contrary lines that may share only the underlying pulse. A loosely enforced pulse may permeate the music, but there may be no standard time signature or subdivision of the beat. This approach sometimes extends to free rhythm, where even the underlying pulse is irregular or completely ignored.

Current sequencer technology provides easy access to syncopation, polyrhythm, and polymeter and can express subtlety in rhythmic feel in a variety of ways. The most notable shortcoming is an inability to improvise. Though technology holds the promise of machine-generated improvisation and has delivered some composing software already, true improvisation is sure to remain a uniquely human capability.

## THE LATIN-AMERICAN TRADITION

The music of Latin America has had a two-sided impact on North American popular music. On one hand, the Latin Americans were the first in the Western Hemisphere to assimilate African rhythms and were vital in fusing these traditions with Western popular music. On the other hand, the native forms and rhythms of Latin music have had their own profound influence on contemporary American and European sounds. In the fifties, the United States was won over by the popular bossa nova, samba, and cha cha dances. All of these employ the standard feel, or meter, of Western music rather than the backbeat, but they bring it to syncopated embellishments and a battery of percussion instruments, both of which have an African ancestry

The bossa nova is the most popular and widely performed of these styles. Its underlying pulse emphasizes beats 1 and 3 and lacks any sort of backbeat accentuation. The bass line in its most basic application reflects this metrical structure.

In popular use, this bass line has been embellished in various ways, using smaller note values to push more strongly onto the accented 1 and 3 beats.

In conjunction with the meter and the bass line, there is a syncopated, two-measure pattern that epitomizes the bossa nova feel. It's a standard clave rhythm and is used in all forms of Latin music. The individual bars in this two-bar phrase may be sometimes be in reverse order.

Combining the clave rhythm with the bass line to form a two-line rhythm yields the following pattern. It occurs with subtle variations in different bossa novas.

Sometimes the clave rhythm is altered slightly so that it becomes an extended series of dotted quarter notes. This is achieved by stretching the last note in the first measure one eighth note beyond its normal position. Two versions of this rhythm are shown below. The first is written in $\frac{4}{4}$; the second is in $\frac{4}{4}$ and shows the full effect of dotted quarter notes in a connected series.

You will remember that the dotted quarter note, when played against a quarter-note pulse, can produce hemiola by imposing a two pulse over three-beat groups. In this case, it is done in $\frac{4}{4}$ time, creating five groups of three eighth notes (or five dotted quarter notes). In the lower example, a single eighth rest is required to fill out the measure.

The bossa nova has crept into jazz, providing a welcome alternative to standard swing and setting up a loose, comfortable groove for improvisation. The prominent use of dotted quarter notes, along with bossa nova bass lines and Latin-American percussion, have added a Latin flavor to numerous instrumentals and popular songs.

Another influential Latin-American form is the samba. It has had a particular impact on American rock and jazz rhythms, and the reason for this is not hard to understand. There are few rhythms in the world that are as exciting as an uptempo samba played on an array of drums and hand percussion, and it provides an ideal setting for soaring, virtuosic improvisation.

The roots of the samba are undoubtedly African as well as Latin-American. In the classic Brazilian or carnival samba, the central rhythm is a two-measure phrase subdivided into eighth notes. The example below is a two-line rhythm usually played on a two-pitched bell or sometimes on two different sized conga drums.

As integrated into American use, this rhythm would be more accurately written in cut-time or as the sixteenth-note rhythm in $\frac{4}{4}$ shown below.

In either case, the samba has a consistent pattern of tension and resolution. The beginning of the rhythm is stable, played on the beat or on simple divisions of it; the middle of the rhythm is unstable, with offbeats creating a very brief polyrhythm; the end of the rhythm returns to the stability of the beat. Thus, we enter and exit the rhythm playing in a stable, pulse-oriented manner, with the interior of the rhythm providing tension. The following examples share this basic characteristic.

Some other popular Latin-American rhythms are shown in the following examples. You may recognize a few of them from their occasional use in pop music, although it's difficult to trace the exact impact of these approaches on current commercial styles. Note that some of these are two-line rhythms and some are three-line rhythms, all indicating multiple drum pitches. An x is used to indicate a rim sound.

## EASTERN TRADITIONS

The ongoing interaction of world cultures, made possible by travel, trade, and communications technology has brought about a fruitful exchange of musical ideas and yielded some intriguing hybrid forms. Popular music is a veritable melting pot of musical and rhythmic influences, blending European harmony with African rhythm and incorporating other elements along the way. The music of the Far East is part of this mixture, contributing unique approaches to timbre, rhythm, and form. Indonesian music has had an interesting, though limited, impact. The gamelan music of Java and Bali, with its interlocking rhythms and a range of drums and metal-lophones, has influenced a number of Western composers working in the jazz and classical idioms. Other Eastern tradi-tions have been absorbed and incorporated into Western approaches in varying degrees, but none have had quite the exposure and impact of the music of India, with its highly developed concept of rhythm and complex system of scales and improvisation.

It is likely that Far Eastern ideas will continue to influence American music, and vice versa, as the world's music continues to become more accessible to all of its inhabitants.

Indian music often employs drums with specific pitch and melodic responsibilities. The primary drum, the tabla, is a hand drum from which pitches are generated through very involved hand and finger muting and stretching of the drum head. The Indian word for rhythm is *tala*, which also refers to specific rhythm patterns that combine to form compositions. The northern and southern Indian traditions are somewhat different, though they also share certain elements. In general, northern *talas* are polymetric, stringing rhythms together in an additive fashion. Southern talas are organized into groups of three and four, called *jatis*, and may be slightly more divisive in concept. A common northern *tala*, called *tintal*, strings together four groups of four beats to form a regular pattern of rhythm. A common southern *tala* uses regular groupings of 4 + 2 + 2. Other *talas*, however, are built on more complex, irregular groups of five and seven. These musical structures, commonly called odd time signatures or "odd times," have found their way into both progressive jazz and classical traditions (think of Dave Brubeck's classic "Take Five") and have even turned up in popular song forms, such as the measures of 7/4 in the Beatles' "All You Need Is Love."

Other elements of Indian music have been employed by jazz, pop, and classical musicians. Free rhythm has been used as a compositional device in both jazz and pop and Indian melodic and harmonic approaches have turned up in the music of the Beatles, John McLaughlin, John Coltrane, and many others. It is likely that Far Eastern ideas will continue to influence American music, and vice versa, as the world's music continues to become more accessible to all of its inhabitants.

*The Rhythm Book*

# PART THREE

# DRUM BEATS IN POPULAR MUSIC

# CHAPTER 8

# A Guide to Use

...the African-derived backbeat dominates the rhythmic structure of all popular styles, from alternative rock to blues and rap, from heavy metal to hip-hop and country. It's what gives the beats their tension and locks together the groove.

From the basics of rhythm and percussion, we now turn to specific beats as they are used in various styles of popular music. For the most part, these are simple models that may be modified and adapted to particular songs and played on traditional percussion instruments or current electronic devices.

Contemporary drum beats reflect a wide diversity of influences in Western popular music. But what ties all these different threads together is the overriding force of the ever-present backbeat. With the exception of Latin-American forms, the African-derived backbeat dominates the rhythmic structure of all popular styles, from alternative rock to blues and rap, from heavy metal to hip-hop and country. It's what gives the beats their tension and locks together the groove. And it will be the starting point for most of the rhythmic patterns covered in this section.

In looking at drum beats used for different pop styles, you'll really be tracing the evolution of the backbeat through varying degrees of complexity. For this reason, it is a good idea to follow an orderly progression through the section, rather than skipping around from chapter to chapter. While it's important to know the special characteristics of individual styles, the fact is that many of these beats are equally at home in a number of different musical settings. By looking at the underlying structure of beats, rather than simply plugging beats into stylistic slots, you'll develop a much more flexible approach to drumming and rhythm playing.

As you progress through these various types and styles of beats, you'll begin to form a larger picture of the way drum beats are constructed; ultimately you'll be able to identify almost any drum beat as a variation or combination of the rhythms shown in these examples. Here you'll begin to gain insight into the overall theory and organization of drumming, beyond just picking up specific beats; you'll approach the goal of thinking like a drummer.

In this section, you'll begin by outlining a basic backbeat pattern as it is played on the drum set, divided among the bass drum, snare, and ride patterns. You'll then take this formula through its application to rock and pop drum beats. As the patterns get more complex, they move into the sophisticated rhythms of contemporary urban styles. By changing the subdivision of the beat while retaining the essential backbeat approach, you'll find yourself in the domain of blues and jazz. Further rhythmic variations yield approaches common to country music and the innovative reggae music. The final style in this section, Latin, is the only one of these forms that does not use the backbeat in its traditional rhythms, although it's quite possible to play patterns that combine a Latin feel within the backbeat approach. Concluding this section are discussions of fills and embellishments, which make use of additional instruments often used with drum set parts and often found on drum machines.

As you progress through these various types and styles of beats, you'll begin to form a larger picture of the way drum beats are constructed; ultimately you'll be able to identify almost any drum beat as a variation or combination of the rhythms shown in these examples. Here you'll begin to gain insight into the overall theory and organization of drumming, beyond just picking up specific beats; you'll approach the goal of thinking like a drummer.

## NOTATING THE DRUM SET

Drum set beats use a very simple system of notation. A standard music stave is used, with different spaces representing different parts of the drum set. Most of the rhythms that you will be looking at will include only a ride pattern (usually played on the closed hi-hat or ride cymbal and written with x's rather than regular note heads), a snare drum rhythm, and a kick (bass) drum rhythm. (For the sake of clarity and true to contemporary recording studio practice, we refer to the bass drum as the kick drum, or simply the kick, to distinguish it from other bass instruments such as bass guitar.) A simple rhythm showing the spaces in the stave used for the ride, snare, and kick is shown below:

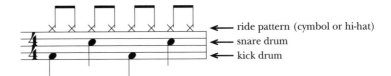

ride pattern (cymbol or hi-hat)
snare drum
kick drum

In later examples, other instruments will be introduced, all of which were first discussed in Chapter Four. They are notated as follows:

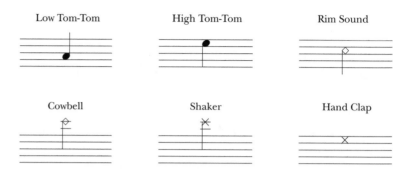

| Low Tom-Tom | High Tom-Tom | Rim Sound |
| Cowbell | Shaker | Hand Clap |

Accenting is indicated by the symbol >. As discussed earlier, variations in accenting will help you achieve a more flexible and loose feel in your drum programming.

## MORE TIPS ON USING THIS SECTION

As you progress through the examples, you will find that the essence of most drum beats boils down to a simple two-line rhythm carried on the kick and snare drums. This basic rhythm has its roots in more primitive instruments that were played with two hands, usually on a single instrument with two relative pitches (e.g.., logs, bells, drums). One hand played a lower pitch and one a higher. In these examples you will also note that the ride pattern has something of an independent function, usually maintaining the pulse.

As you grow more comfortable with these beats and with rhythm work in general, you should begin to create your own beats that are similar to the patterns shown in any given category.

Many of these examples are expressed in one-, two-, and four-measure patterns. These lengths tend to be the best building blocks for composing drum parts. As you grow more comfortable with these beats and with rhythm work in general, you should begin to create your own beats that are similar to the patterns shown in any given category. One way to do this is to extract single measures from some of the longer patterns and then recombine them in new ways.

If you play an instrument other than drums, you'll find that an awareness of the beats in this section will help out when you're working with a drummer or programming drum parts in a sequencer. You might also try playing some of these rhythms on your own instrument. From two-note rhythms to chordal rhythm parts, there are numerous ways to interpret drum set rhythms on any instrument. Players who are involved with programming will probably want to use many of these beat patterns as they begin to program different rhythm ideas for their music.

Whatever your involvement in rhythm, keep experimenting and trying different things. And remember: there's a good reason why musical activity is called "playing." Enjoy it.

# CHAPTER 9

# Rock and Pop

Current rock and pop music, as discussed earlier, really encompasses a broad spectrum of approaches. While the dynamics and timbre of rhythm tracks may differ depending on the style—powerful and full-bodied for hard rock or somewhat more restrained and colorful for melodic pop—the underlying beat patterns are quite similar.

We have already set the stage for the following examples by establishing the importance of the backbeat in popular music and by tracing the evolution of the modern drum set. At this point you have a clear understanding of the backbeat and are familiar with the basic parts of a set of drums. Now we'll look at the way those two essential elements combine to form some of the relatively simple patterns used in rock music.

## THE BACKBEAT ON THE DRUM SET

The following example shows a basic backbeat as played on the drum set. Two critical functions are accomplished in this simple example. The top line, or ride pattern (played most commonly on the closed hi-hat), sets up the eighth-note pulse. The kick drum and the snare drum form a two-line rhythm that presents the backbeat in its simplest form.

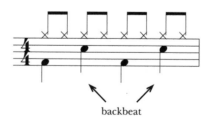

backbeat

In this example, the two-line rhythm formed by kick and snare drums is actually a simple quarter-note pulse—the primary beats. You will remember from our discussions of meter and the backbeat that the backbeat sets up a kind of call and response relationship. This is created by answering the kick drum (beats 1 and 3) with the snare drum (beats 2 and 4). The backbeat answers back, providing the meter with a kind of built-in tension. Although the kick/snare rhythm is a simple pulse, the contrast between the two sounds—the big bass boom of the kick drum and the sharp crack of the snare drum—underscores a distinct metric feel, evolved from two-handed rhythms.

The simplest extension of the backbeat model adds rhythmic interest by adding to the kick drum pattern, as seen in the following examples. These drum beats maintain all of the elements in our original model: the eighth-note pulse in the ride pattern, the kick on the 1 and 3, and the backbeat, or beats 2 and 4, on the snare drum. In addition, they develop the two-line rhythm created by developing the kick snare pattern beyond the basic quarter-note pulse. Starting with our original backbeat model, we begin thinking about the space between each kick and snare beat (each quarter note of the measure). Our ride-pattern pulse fills in each space with an additional eighth note beat, called the "and" beat. Each of these "and" beats provide a place for an additional kick drum beat. In one measure of $\frac{4}{4}$ time there are four of these "and" beats, called the "and of 1" following the 1-beat, the "and of 2," the "and of 3," and the "and of 4". Each of these "and" beats may have a kick drum beat or not. Remember that these beats still include the kick drum on the 1 and 3 beats and the snare on the 2 and 4, so that the quarter-note pulse remains a part of the two-line snare/kick rhythm.

Using these "and" beat options for the kick drum enables you to create many of the basic drum beats found in a large number of contemporary songs. You might recognize the second example above as the beat played by Ringo in the introduction to (and throughout most of) the Beatles song "Sgt. Pepper's Lonely Hearts Club Band." Literally thousands of songs use these basic drum beats—or similar ones—through the majority of the song or in particular sections.

Remember that accenting is indicated by the mark shown above the ride pattern. The primary beats carry an accent, while the "and" beats are unaccented. The accent applies to the kick and the snare beats as well as the ride pattern. The use of accenting is very important in establishing the feel in these rhythms.

## DEVELOPING THE SNARE DRUM

As seen in the next example, you may also use the "and" counts for additional snare beats. Here proper accenting is crucial in bringing out the backbeats. While used quite frequently, these patterns are less common than the simple kick drum rhythms already developed. This is probably because, even with proper accenting, any additional snare beats can draw away from the simple backbeat feel.

*The Rhythm Book*

There are other ways to expand the basic backbeat. In the previous examples, you maintained either kick or snare statements on all four of the primary beats. In the next example, you'll eliminate the kick drum from beat 3. This creates a syncopation because beat 3, which is one of the primary beats, is no longer played in the two-line rhythm created by the kick/snare pattern.

...the 3 beat is the least important of the four primary beats.

This is the most common type of primary beat syncopation because the 1-beat is the most important beat (and center of both rhythmic arrival and departure), and beats 2 and 4 create the backbeat. Thus the 3 beat is the least important of the four primary beats. It serves as a secondary 1-beat and helps to distinguish the four-beat cycle (quadruple meter) from the two-beat cycle (duple meter). By not playing the kick at this poin,t you emphasize the importance of the 1-beat and thus give additional importance to the cycle of four, as you now must return to the 1-beat to resolve the cycle.

This rhythm has a syncopated sound and feel even though the ride pattern plays a continuous pulse that includes every primary beat. The pulse-keeping function of the ride pattern should be thought of separately from the two-line rhythm created by the kick/snare pattern.

Other patterns use different approaches to the three-beat syncopation. Note that both the kick and the snare drum parts are developed below, though rhythmic interest is provided mostly by the kick drum. The two-measure rhythm uses the 3-beat syncopation only in the second measure. A typical use of this type of beat might be as a pattern in the verse of a song, with the chorus releasing to one of the more basic beats, as in the Rolling Stones classic "Honky-Tonk Woman."

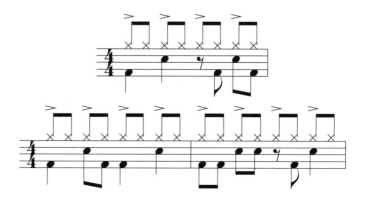

## ALTERING THE RIDE PATTERN

The pulse-keeping function of the ride pattern may be altered from the standard eighth-note pulse you have used up until now. While the eighth-note pulse is most common, other divisions of the pulse may also be used. In the following example, the ride pattern is reduced to quarter notes, sounding only on the primary beats. Meanwhile, the kick and snare rhythm is a version of one of our earlier patterns. This ride pattern is most appropriate for faster tempos and/or within sparser arrangements. As with almost all ride patterns, this one is played on the closed hi-hat, though it may also be played on the ride cymbal. Occasionally, other instruments such as cowbell, woodblock, or even tom-tom may substitute here in place of cymbals.

The next examples demonstrate ride patterns appropriate to slower and faster tempos, using kick and snare beats familiar from previous examples. The double-time ride pattern is common in slower tempos and ballads. With the use of sixteen notes per measure, the accenting function becomes increasingly important in maintaining the sense of the primary beats—the quarter-note pulse. If you are playing this beat on the drums or programming it in a sequencers try putting the strongest accent on the primary beats, a secondary accent on the "and" beats, and an unaccented note on the intermediary sixteenth notes (the "e" and "a" beats).

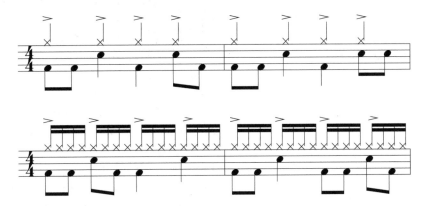

## HOW DOES ROCK RHYTHM DIFFER FROM POP?

So far, we've discussed rock and pop as one category, without distinguishing between the two. The fact is that in terms of rhythm structure, the drum beats you have looked at here would be as likely to appear in one style as in the other, the two being very closely related. The differences between rock and pop can be heard more in the way the drums sound on a finished recording than in the patterns actually played. In classic rock, the drums are likely to be featured more, mixed more loudly in relation to the other instruments and voice, than they are on a pop record. Rock drums are usually played more forcefully and there will usually be more fills than in a normal pop drum arrangement. But a basic backbeat approach and simple rhythms are equally common to both styles.

Many artists may defy this somewhat arbitrary distinction between rock and pop. Keep in mind also that these types of basic, backbeat-oriented beats may be used in virtually every style of contemporary music, though perhaps less frequently than in rock and pop styles.

# R&B, Funk, Rap, and Hip Hop

Notice how all of
these examples may
be understood as
substituting for the
backbeat rather than
simply omitting it.

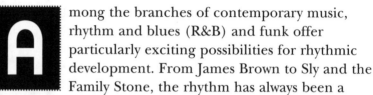 mong the branches of contemporary music, rhythm and blues (R&B) and funk offer particularly exciting possibilities for rhythmic development. From James Brown to Sly and the Family Stone, the rhythm has always been a prominent feature of this sound and has been the testing ground for innovations in structure, instrumental technique, and electronics. These styles have provided much of the groundwork for the more contemporary urban styles of rap and hip-hop that we will discuss at the end of this chapter.

By further developing the backbeat rhythms that were introduced in the previous chapter, we can create rhythms that are common to the sounds of R&B and funk. Again there is a lot of overlapping of rhythms in contemporary music, and as important as it is to recognize differences in style, it is equally important to follow the evolution of rhythms and see how they are related. Notice that you can simplify these drum beats just a bit and they become the same beats discussed in the previous chapter—though the rhythms are more complex, the backbeat remains prominent.

...the kick drum provides most of the rhythmic interest in common drum set patterns.

You have already seen that the kick drum provides most of the rhythmic interest in common drum set patterns. Here we take this further by introducing a sixteenth-note subdivision of the beat.

Notice that the kick-drum beats no longer necessarily correspond to all the pulse beats in the eighth-note ride pattern. In the example we have added the sixteenth note prior to beat 3 (the "a" of beat 2) to our basic backbeat rhythm. In this case, the sixteenth note is a simple push beat on to beat 3, more of an embellishment than a syncopation. The most common rhythmic use of sixteenth notes is as embellishment beats, usually pushing on to either the kick or the snare, on one or more of the primary beats.

...it is useful to think of these beats without the additional sixteenth notes and see how they have been developed from the basic rhythms you saw in the previous chapter.

Opening up the drum rhythm to sixteenth notes can be important to the drummer's ability to support other instruments and to create fills and embellishments. This particular drum beat could serve in either a simple or complex musical environment.

The next examples elaborate on the use of the sixteenth note in the kick drum part, primarily as an embellishment beat. Again, it is useful to think of these beats without the additional sixteenth notes and see how they have been developed from the basic rhythms you saw in the previous chapter.

When you use more complex rhythms such as these, you'll want to pay particular attention to accenting. The additional sixteenth notes are usually played more quietly, which is appropriate for an embellishment. The primary beats will carry the primary accents, the "and" beats will be played more quietly, and the "e" and "a" beats more quietly still.

The following shows a sixteenth-note kick drum beat used independent of a primary beat. As in our initial example, you play the "a" of 2, but this time the kick does not play the following 3-beat. This kind of use creates a syncopated-feeling rhythm. It either feels as if the sixteenth-note is left hanging, or as if the 3-beat has been anticipated (played early).

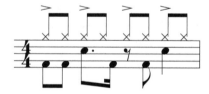

Drum beats such as this are common in the broad style often called funk. Funk can include both progressive pop and jazz styles. It has also been characterized by the slap bass guitar sound, which, through a special right-hand slapping technique, produces a twangy popping sound that interacts closely with the drums. Note that the type of funky syncopation in the rhythm above is most likely to take place around the 3-beat, just as you saw in our initial rock syncopation. Again, this is because the 3-beat is the least important of the four primary beats.

Next are more examples of syncopated sixteenth-note subdivisions within the backbeat context. Care must be taken in using these rhythms because they will tend to dominate a musical situation. They leave little room for other rhythmic ideas or counterpoint.

## DEVELOPING THE SNARE—SIXTEENTH NOTES AND SUBSTITUTE BACKBEATS

**Snare drum embellishments are especially good for adding to a feeling of rhythmic motion.**

You can use sixteenth notes with the snare drum just as you did with the kick drum. The snare continues to provide the accented backbeat, with the embellishment beats commonly unaccented.

Snare drum embellishments are especially good for adding to a feeling of rhythmic motion. Often snare embellishments such as these are really very short fills that connect larger song sections. As in the previous kick drum examples, these additional snare beats occasionally fall between pulse beats in the ride pattern.

Notice that you can simplify these drum beats just a bit and they become the same beats discussed in the previous chapter—though the rhythms are more complex, the backbeat remains prominent.

Here are some snare examples that actually pull the snare off of one of the two backbeats. The first example, similar to what Ringo Starr used in the Beatles' "Tomorrow Never Knows," shows an accented snare beat on the "and" of 3, with no snare on the 4-beat. You might call this a *substitute backbeat* because this "and of 3" beat is fulfilling the normal backbeat function, though not in the normal location. Notice how all of these examples may be understood as substituting for the backbeat rather than simply omitting it.

It is more common to substitute for the 4-beat than the 2-beat because the change occurs later in the measure and is less disruptive to the overall rhythm. In certain cases, substitutions may be on either the "and" beats or on the sixteenth note "e" and "a" beats. The concept of substitute backbeat provides a means of creating highly syncopated rhythms that retain the basic form of the contemporary backbeat pattern.

The interaction between the snare drum and the kick drum provides the primary focus in all of the drum set rhythms examined so far. The following examples combine the use of sixteenth-note subdivisions in both the kick and the snare, creating an even more pronounced interaction between the two. The ride pattern retains the simple accented eighth-note pulse.

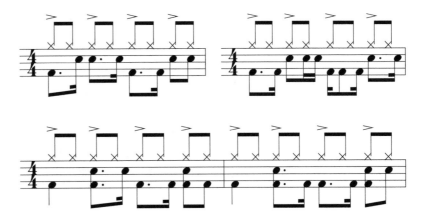

> **By thinking of these and most all drum patterns as kick/snare conversations, you gain insight into the way a drummer usually expresses the natural feeling of playing a drum set. It encourages you to think of the drum set as a single instrument, rather than as a group of distinct sounds.**

There are only two levels of accenting indicated in these examples, though busy beats such as these would benefit from more subtle degrees of accentuation. Whether you are playing these beats or programming them, you should experiment with subtle shifts of volume throughout the beat. Generally, you will want to use a diminishing volume scale, moving from louder to softer from the primary beats to the "and" beats to the "e" and "a" beats.

By thinking of these and most all drum patterns as kick/snare conversations, you gain insight into the way a drummer usually expresses the natural feeling of playing a drum set. It encourages you to think of the drum set as a single instrument, rather than as a group of distinct sounds.

Any of the examples discussed so far could use different pulse rates for the ride patterns, as in the examples below. Quarter-note ride patterns will work, but sixteenth-note rides would be more common in these contexts, coinciding with sixteenth-note subdivisions in the kick and snare.

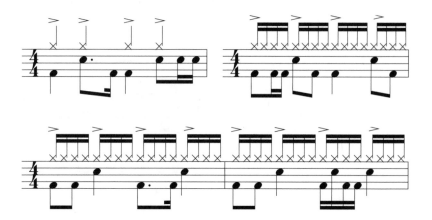

In the next example, we have provided a simple and familiar kick/snare pattern while breaking up the straight pulse-keeping function of the ride. Here the ride rhythm is adjusted so that all the notes in the eighth-note pulse are still played, yet the "and" beats are divided into two sixteenth notes. The resulting three-note combinations (not to be confused with triplets) maintain a strong sense of beat and provide increased movement.

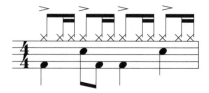

Note that the three-note combinations push from the "and" beats on to the primary beats, emphasizing the quarter-note pulse. This is especially useful in faster tempos that still call for a double-time feeling. The Stevie Wonder hit "Superstitious" employs this kind of ride pattern (played, as is typical, on the closed hi-hat). Three-note combinations working in the other direction (from the primary pulse to an "and" beat) would not provide as strong or propulsive a rhythm.

In the following examples, the ride is shown playing a more independent and less pulse-oriented rhythm. This expands the beat into a three-line rhythm since the ride pattern is interacting with the kick/snare pattern as an equal or even more developed part of the overall sound. These types of drum beats are heard most often in various jazz-tinged styles as well as in certain Latin-influenced approaches.

By using this three-line approach to drumming, you can begin to see how some very complex rhythms can be developed. The key to making them work is to listen to the combined effect of the three lines, as well as to each independent part, making sure that they work together as a whole. When playing complicated ride patterns it is advisable to keep the kick and snare parts simple. That way you'll avoid an overly busy drum part that diverts attention from the music as a whole (unless you're playing a drum solo that is looking for attention).

## RAP AND HIP-HOP

Today's urban music landscape is filled with cross-fertilized genres that involve whole new techniques of creating music. Rap and hip-hop music are at the forefront in using these new techniques, especially those that use sampled drum and rhythm parts from previously existing songs to create new grooves. Early rap artists were the first to embrace drum machines and sequenced drum parts as an accepted standard, and the art of DJ scratching added new and unique rhythmic elements to basic rhythm tracks. Contemporary rap and hip-hop may integrate techniques involving sequencing, sampling, looping, and scratching with or without traditional drum tracks. Early rap tracks tended to be tied to one simple groove, often created using a sequencer and containing virtually no

**Contemporary rap and hip-hop may integrate techniques involving sequencing, sampling, looping, and scratching with or without traditional drum tracks.**

advanced programming techniques such as accenting or time shifting, let alone any variations on the groove or fills between sections. Contemporary rap and hip-hop tracks may adhere to this earlier formula or they may incorporate a full range of rhythmic subtlety through advanced programming techniques as well as many other techniques developed within this genre. General rhythmic approaches also run the full gamut, from the most basic kind of rock beat to highly syncopated funk type rhythms. In a later chapter we will focus on the innovative rhythmic approaches that this genre has spawned, though its adoption and development of techniques was only made possible with the advent of digital sound and computer-based manipulation of rhythm.

# Blues and Jazz

Blues and jazz employ shuffle and swing rhythms, in which the primary beats are divided into threes (triplets).

n the previous drum beat examples reflecting basic approaches to playing rock and funk, we divided our primary quarter-note beat in twos (eighth-notes) and fours (sixteenth notes). Blues and jazz employ shuffle and swing rhythms, in which the primary beats are divided into threes (triplets). Shuffle and swing beats also bring up the important question of *feel*, which lies at the basis of all rhythm and will be discussed more thoroughly in a later chapter. For now, let's take a look at some of the standard patterns used in this music.

## THE SHUFFLE

The basic shuffle beat is expressed in the ride pattern in the following example. The first and third notes in each triplet (the downbeat and "ta" beat) are sounded to create the shuffle feel. This is almost like playing straight eighth notes except with a lazier approach to the "and" beat so that it occurs later in time, becoming a triplet "ta" beat rather than an "and" beat. In this example, the kick and snare play the most basic backbeat pattern. As in previous examples, the downbeat is accented and the intermediary notes are unaccented.

Apart from being used in the blues, the shuffle beat has been applied to rock and has provided a powerful, rolling, forward momentum to many songs in that style. Bruce Springsteen used it successfully in "Kitty's Back," as did Billy Ocean in his number one hit, "When the Going Gets Tough (The Tough Get Going)." Tears for Fears also applied it to their number one song, "Everybody Wants to Rule the World."

Since the shuffle rhythm is an adaptation—a more developed version of a straight eighth-note pulse—it's easy to adapt any of the all-eighth-note ride examples from the basic backbeat rhythm to shuffle beats, such as those in the examples below. The backbeat feel remains intact.

## THE ⁶⁄₈ BLUES RHYTHM

A slow version of the shuffle beat, with all the triplets in the ride filled in, is usually written in ⁶⁄₈ as shown next. This approach has become something of a style in itself, sometimes referred to as "slow blues," and it is used in such classic tunes as "Stormy Monday" and "Spoonful." The ⁶⁄₈ time signature has two groups of three eighth notes in each measure. Although not written as triplets, the effect is an even more pronounced feeling of groups of three than in the basic shuffle. The kick and snare drums provide rhythms very similar to the shuffle beat within this framework, only slower. The snare drum still provides a backbeat (the 4 beat in ⁶⁄₈ time), despite the time signature.

The following examples are additional versions of $^6_8$ beats. Note that in the first example we have created kick and snare sixteenth-note embellishments in a few places. In the second example, the ride pattern is subdivided into sixteenth-note triplets. When done simply in a slow tempo, this very small subdivision may sound quite smooth and comfortable. We will look a bit more into this kind of sixteenth-note triplet subdivision in the final section of this chapter.

## THE SWING BEAT

The basic rhythm of traditional jazz is called *swing*. The format is the same as the shuffle beat, though the basic ride rhythm is slightly more sparse. In swing, the "ta" beat is only played prior to the 1- and 3-beats. This makes the ride rhythm closer to a simple quarter-note pulse, creating a less defined and more spacious environment than the shuffle pattern. Here the kick and snare are creating the basic backbeat rhythm, appropriate to dance-oriented forms of jazz prevalent in the thirties (like the music played by Benny Goodman and Tommy Dorsey). Steady rhythms such as this one tended to reinforce the pulse created by the traditional "walking" melody played on string bass.

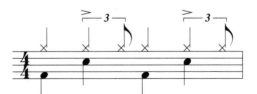

As jazz developed, the snare became used more for embellishment, though the sense of backbeat was generally maintained. In the following examples the kick and snare are syncopated, and both jobs of pulse keeping and backbeat accenting are maintained by the ride pattern. The 2- and 4-beats in the ride pattern carry a stronger accent than the 1- or 3-beats, with the intermediary triplets remaining unaccented. Note the frequent use of the "ta" beats played on kick and snare. These beats anticipate the downbeat, providing an offbeat rhythmic feel; they often coincide with accents played on rhythm instruments such as guitar or piano.

Syncopation is often referred to as the hallmark of jazz and, within that context, has reached new peaks of complexity. Jazz drummers have applied complex syncopations in both written and improvised situations. Among the best known "mainstream" jazz innovators are Max Roach, Elvin Jones, and Buddy Rich.

## DEVELOPING SWING AND THE SHUFFLE

We might call the next example a bass/snare conversation in swing rhythm. Here the kick/snare parts complete some of the triplets, including the second or "ti" notes. In the form shown, the kick plays the primary beat while the snare fills in the middle "ti" and "ta" beats.

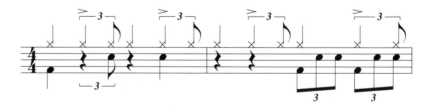

The following examples show the use of a triplet or shuffle subdivision on the sixteenth-note level, requiring sixteenth-note triplets (as we saw in one of the $\frac{6}{8}$ blues beats). Here the triplets are used within the context of a backbeat and an eighth-note ride. These triplets may occur in the kick, snare, or ride patterns, or in combinations of any of the three. The basic conventions of accenting, maintenance of the backbeat, and orientation toward kick/snare conversations apply to these patterns as they did to earlier beats.

These rhythms have been used in many styles of pop music. Groups such as The Band in rock and The Crusaders in jazz have reached large audiences with material that employs this approach. Contemporary rap and hip-hop artists have also frequently used this kind of triplet subdivision within a backbeat model.

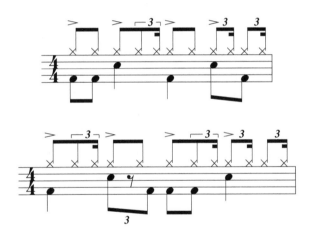

# Country, Reggae, and Latin

In this chapter, we will look at a particular kind of traditional country music beat: the two-beat rhythm, generally written in what is called cut time.

Reggae's intriguing hybrid of backbeat and two-beat rhythms is examined in this section.

Traditional Latin styles have enjoyed great popularity and influence in American pop music since the fifties, with the modern bossa nova and samba dances attracting particular attention. Among the interesting aspects of these dances is that they do not use the backbeat as a rhythmic device.

The tremendous cross-fertilization of popular music's various styles makes it difficult to generalize too much about rhythmic convention. In fact, it is more and more difficult to pigeonhole a song or composition according to one style. The result of this style mixing is that today basic rhythm patterns can be used in different forms of music. In this chapter, we'll look at three distinctive styles: country, reggae, and Latin.

Country music is an idiom that has both exerted tremendous influence on, and in turn been greatly influenced, by rock and pop styles. The drum set rhythms outlined in the rock and pop section are almost as common in today's country and folk music. In this chapter, we will look at a particular kind of traditional country music beat: the two-beat rhythm, generally written in what is called *cut time*.

Reggae, a fairly recent addition to U.S. radio airwaves, is one of the more distinctive strains of pop music. At the root of reggae's uniqueness is its rhythmic structure as played on a drum set. Bob Marley's work exemplifies the classic reggae tradition, while the Police, in much of their music, managed to blend reggae rhythms into a more traditional pop song structure. Reggae's intriguing hybrid of backbeat and two-beat rhythms is examined in this section.

Traditional Latin styles have enjoyed great popularity and influence in American pop music since the fifties, with the modern bossa nova and samba dances attracting particular attention. Among the interesting aspects of these dances is that they do not use the backbeat as a rhythmic device. The rhythms, in fact, are felt on the 1- and 3-beats, just as in the Western classical tradition.

One of the more common rhythmic structures used in country music is called cut-time. On a page of music, cut-time (or *alla breve* in classical music) looks identical to $\frac{4}{4}$ time except that the time signature is given a ¢. In cut-time we feel the beat on the 1- and 3-beats of a four-beat bar rather than on all four primary beats. The rhythm is basically felt in $\frac{2}{2}$ (two half-note beats to the bar), but it is counted in $\frac{4}{4}$. It differs from $\frac{2}{4}$ in that we want to consider all four quarter notes as beats, but we only want to feel two of them. The traditional cut-time carries the backbeat on the 2- and 4-beats, though they are not as prominent as in rock and pop. The traditional foot stomp followed by the hand clap indicates the appropriate feel of a two-beat, cut-time rhythm (also called an "oom-pah" beat). A quickness of the tempo is important in establishing the snappy two-beat feeling.

Below you see the same two-beat rhythm using a shuffle or triplet division of the beat rather than the straight eighth notes we saw in the first example. In both examples, notice that the ride pattern is not a strict pulse but uses an embellishment beat to move the rhythm on to beat 3 and then back to beat 1.

Next are some simple variations on the basic two-beat approach. The drum set accompaniment in country music is generally very simple, in keeping with a straightforward lyric and melodic approach.

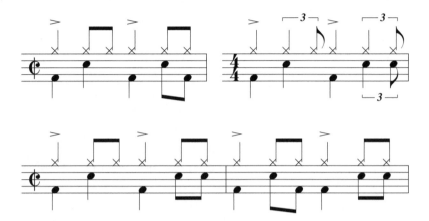

## REGGAE

Reggae, largely a Jamaican distillation of American rhythm and blues, has a distinctive approach to rhythm characterized by shifting accents and surprising spaces where one would normally expect a sound or a beat.

Reggae, largely a Jamaican distillation of American rhythm and blues, has a distinctive approach to rhythm characterized by shifting accents and surprising spaces where one would normally expect a sound or a beat. The following example illustrates the essence of the most exciting of the reggae rhythmic innovations on the drum set. The kick/snare pattern is the most basic of backbeats, and the ride pattern is a simple quarter-note pulse. The difference, however, is that the ride pattern has been displaced one eighth note so that the quarter-note pulse is played on the "and" beats rather than on the primary beats.

We could think of this rhythm as two bars of cut-time, with the ride pattern forming an answer beat against the pulse of the kick and snare. The subtle two-beat jumpiness, overlaid on a basic backbeat structure, creates an exciting new rhythm that is not only characteristic of reggae, but has also been used in virtually every other style of popular music in the last decade.

*The Rhythm Book*

Reggae rhythms of this kind can become a blanket of interwoven accents, combining various feels with implied beats and overlapping pulses.

Another reggae innovation, though less original than the last, is shown in the following example. Here the drums omit the 1-beat—the central beat of the bar. This omission is not quite as drastic as it may sound when listened to alone, because in a band setting the bass guitar part will usually still land very strongly on beat 1. Without the normal reinforcement of the kick drum, this provides an unusual feeling of lightness and suspension.

Next, the basic reggae approach is developed to include a double-time feel in addition to the overlaid backbeat and two-beat rhythms. The sixteenth-note pattern in the ride maintains the two-beat jump while introducing a sixteenth-note subdivision. The kick and snare patterns may include sixteenth-note embellishment beats. Reggae rhythms of this kind can become a blanket of interwoven accents, combining various feels with implied beats and overlapping pulses.

The traditional Latin dance form, the bossa nova, came to prominence in the U.S. in the early sixties with the Stan Getz-Astrud Gilberto collaboration ("The Girl from Ipanema"), further entered the popular consciousness through the songs of Antonio Carlos Jobim, and today is an essential rhythmic component of jazz and the occasional rock song. It has come to be commonly interpreted on the drum set as a two-bar rhythm as illustrated here. The diamond-shaped notes indicate the rim sound—a sound created by placing the tip of the drum stick against the snare drum head and hitting the back end of the stick against the rim of the drum. This technique, called cross-sticking, creates a clicking effect similar to the traditional hardwood sound of claves. The rhythm in this example has the claves part used in much traditional Latin-American music, played here using the cross-sticking technique. This trademark syncopation is distinguished by its prominent use of the dotted quarter-note (a quarter-note plus an eighth-note in duration).

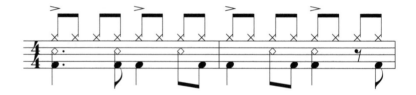

The bossa nova rhythm does not employ the backbeat. The underlying accents are felt only on beats 1 and 3. In the standard kick-drum pattern shown, the "and" beats preceding beats 1 and 3 provide movement on to the accented primary beats.

In the next examples, a new drum is introduced: the tom-tom (hi-tom). It is shown in the top space of the staff. These examples represent two variations of the bossa nova rhythm. The first example is the same as the previous one, except that it reverses the rim or claves rhythm, placing the second measure first. This is a common variation on the traditional form. In the second example, the rhythm is embellished with tom-tom accents. Every rim beat is answered by the hi-tom on the following eighth note. The very end of the rhythm has also been altered, increasing the use of dotted quarter note equivalents. The tom-tom rhythm provides a kind of echo or shadow effect. Experiment with the dotted quarter notes in the clave rhythm when creating other bossa nova–type rhythms. Notice that kick drum accents are used here, shown in the space just above the kick drum note. Also bear in mind that the hi-tom is played with the left hand (an obvious point when you note that the right-hand ride pattern is maintained throughout these rhythms).

low-tom →

## LATIN—SAMBA

The samba, an uptempo, exciting Latin-American dance form, traveled from Brazil to the U.S. via popular musicians like Baden Powell, Milton Nascimento, Airto Moreira, and Gilberto Gil. It has been used extensively in jazz, especially in the flashier, colorful fusion branches of the music.

The following pattern shows the modern drum set interpretation of the traditional samba rhythm. It includes the addition of a low tom-tom (low-tom), which is shown on the second space of the staff, between the kick and the snare. The samba is written and felt in cut-time, as were the traditional country rhythms explored earlier. With the samba, however, there is no backbeat and there is a much higher degree of syncopation. The samba phrase is also a two-bar rhythm. The feeling of the beat could be accurately represented by condensing one of these two-measure patterns into a one-measure pattern that is subdivided by sixteenth notes rather than eighths. In keeping with the cut-time approach, the traditional samba tempo is quick. If you play or program this rhythm at a slow tempo and gradually increase the tempo rate, you can feel the rhythm gradually change from a cumbersome four-beat feel into the light and proper two-beat feel of cut-time.

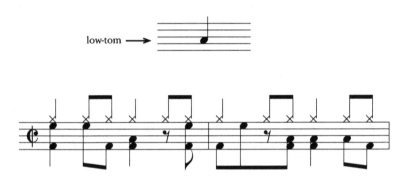

Next, the high- and low-tom patterns are altered for rhythmic interest. Note that the kick and ride patterns remain constant.

An interesting tendency in this kind of tom-tom rhythm (often heard in syncopated two-bar rhythms, which are discussed in Chapter 7) is that the first few beats of the first measure and the last few beats of the second measure tend to be more stable parts of the rhythm. The middle part, on the other hand, including the end of measure 1 and the beginning of measure 2, tends to be the place for most of the syncopation. You can think of the overall rhythm as starting and ending with stability on the primary beats, with the tension created by syncopation sandwiched in between. The process of instability leading to stability or tension to resolution is an essential source of motion in music and rhythm. It is helpful to keep it in mind when analyzing or composing rhythms.

A different approach to the samba is shown in the next example. The kick, rim, and tom-toms are used to set up a basic two-beat pulse, and the typical samba rhythm is played in the ride pattern. This ride pattern is often played on the bell of a cymbal, imitating the sound of a cowbell.

# CHAPTER 13

# Embellishments and Fills

**R**are is the pop song that relies solely on the kick-snare-ride patterns discussed so far. Today's rhythm tracks on pop recordings and in live performances include an array of embellishments and fills that serve to fill out the basic beat patterns, add excitement and propulsion to the music, and signal transitions into new sections of a song. While these variations on basic rhythms are often played on the instruments observed so far—the kick and snare drums, ride cymbal, hi hat, and tom-toms—they may also come from other percussion that expand the palette of drum sounds. Now that we've explored the realm of standard beats in several pop styles, we can move into a discussion of these embellishments and the additional percussion instruments on which they may be played. In addition, the libraries of synths and samplers contain an assortment of sounds that are well-suited for rhythmic fills and variations.

In the last chapter, you used the tom-toms to create certain typical Latin rhythms. Here you'll expand the use of tom-toms in a variety of other ways. You'll also develop the use of the hi-hat, creating a distinctive metallic "sizzle" sound by opening and closing the two cymbals. Other sounds found or simulated on a drum set, added by a percussionist, or included in most synth and sampler libraries are the rim sound, cowbell, shaker, crash cymbal, and hand claps.

The term drum fill comes from the idea of a "fill-in" part in which the drummer plays a busier or louder phrase to move the music from the end of one section of music to the beginning of another.

The term *drum fill* comes from the idea of a "fill-in" part in which the drummer plays a busier or louder phrase to move the music from the end of one section of music to the beginning of another. Now drum fills are used quite frequently for a variety of purposes, such as embellishing a musical phrase or building excitement under a guitar solo. Since the possibilities for fills are as unlimited as the imagination of each individual percussionist, it would be impossible to offer here a complete list of standard embellishments. Instead, you should use this discussion as a jumping off point for further exploration, keeping in mind that ultimately it will be your ear that tells you what is appropriate in the music you're working on.

## TOM-TOMS

Tom-toms allow numerous ways to create rhythmic and tonal interest in drum beats. Many drum sets have three or four tom-toms available with which to expand the tonal variety of any rhythm you happen to be creating.

The following four patterns employ two tom-toms in different ways. In the first pattern, the toms are simply used to double the snare drum on the backbeat, creating a thicker backbeat sound. The second pattern uses the toms as though they were a part of the kick drum pattern, thereby providing variation in timbre. The third pattern uses them within the context of kick/snare conversations, again providing tonal variety. The final pattern shows the floor-tom (low-tom) used as the sound for the basic ride pattern, with the eighth-note pulse shown in x's on the floor-tom line. Experiment with substituting toms for cymbals in various ride patterns, but notice how dense this makes the rhythm. Because of its density or bottom heaviness, this approach should be used sparingly. One possible use is to build up to an instrumental solo over several measures, increasing volume as you approach the downbeat of the solo. In heavy rock music, tom-toms are used more extensively due to the dense "wall of sound" quality of that kind of music.

## OPEN AND CLOSED HI-HAT

It is the unique nature of the hi-hat that it can be played open (by leaving the foot off the hi-hat pedal) and closed (by stepping down on the pedal), allowing for a variety of sounds. An open hi-hat produces a sustained cymbal sound as the two hi-hat cymbals continue to vibrate against each other. The sustain is cut off when the hi-hat closes again or when the vibration stops. (To reproduce this effect with a synth or sampler, it is usually necessary to program a closed hi-hat note at the point you wish to stop the open hi-hat.)

In notation, a tie is used to indicate an open hi-hat beat, which is sustained from the beginning of the tie to the end. The sound will stop at the next closed hi-hat beat.

The closed hi-hat is the most common instrument used for playing the ride pattern. The opening and closing of the hi-hat at certain points in the ride pattern can add a new dimension of sound to your rhythm creations. These examples indicate common uses of the open hi-hat combined with the closed hi-hat within familiar patterns.

## RIM SOUND

The sound that is generally labeled rim on a drum machine or within a drum sound library is actually the sound of what drummers call *cross-sticking*. This means placing the stick's tip on the drum head and then striking the rim of the drum with the butt end of the stick. It's different from a rim shot, which is a loud sound created by striking the rim and the head of the drum simultaneously.

The rim sound is especially useful in the bossa nova and other Latin rhythms, as it approaches the sound of the wooden claves. Because of its high-pitched, clicking sound, it may also be used as a replacement for the snare drum. The examples below use the rim sound in a few typical beats. These are likely to be used in slower tempos, providing a quieter feeling overall than the use of the snare drum. The rim sound is notated as a diamond shaped note.

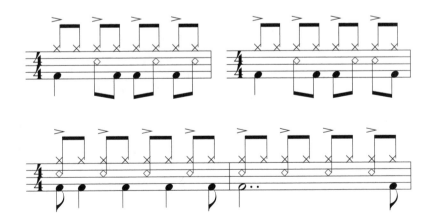

The cowbell has been put to considerable use in almost all kinds of popular music, though it is especially evident in Latin-American or Latin-influenced styles. It may serve as an addition to or replacement for the ride pattern, as it has the frequency range of cymbals (but a fuller sound) and, like the closed hi-hat, no real sustain. Simple cowbell patterns may supplement hi-hat ride patterns in rock and roll, while complex cowbell syncopation may add spice to dance music in all styles. The follwoing examples show some simple uses of the cowbell, which is written on the second ledger line above the ride pattern.

Another instrument in the high frequency range is the shaker, which is often used in direct relationship to hi-hat and/or cymbal ride patterns. It may be used to duplicate the ride pattern, adding texture to the sound. Doubling the ride pattern has an additional benefit in the recording process: it allows you to set up the pattern in stereo by placing the hi-hat on the left channel and the shaker on the right. You can also use the shaker to replace the ride pattern, as in the following two-bar example , or to play an independent idea. As with playing or programming all drum parts, accenting serves an important role in giving the shaker parts a natural feel. In these examples, the shaker is notated as an x on the second ledger line above the ride pattern.

## HAND CLAPS

Clapping has a long tradition in popular music, but the availability of claps as samples has made this sound a much more prominent part of many current recordings. (The sound and number of claps in the sample may vary considerably.) Claps are most commonly used to reinforce the backbeats along with the snare or sometimes to replace the snare. The third example here uses claps within a fill.

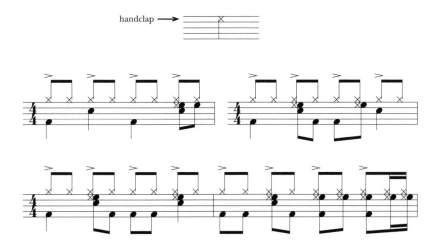

Not every (or even
necessarily any)
transition needs to be
marked with a drum fill,
but it can be a very
effective way to create
a strong feeling of
movement and arrival.

Fills are generally used to mark musical transitions, such as a verse moving to a chorus, a chorus to a bridge, an instrumental to a chorus, and so on. Not every (or even necessarily any) transition needs to be marked with a drum fill, but it can be a very effective way to create a strong feeling of movement and arrival.

The following four fills just scratch the surface of available ideas. The kick drum may or may not play through a fill, depending on what sounds most natural. Normally, the ride will stop during a fill, as the drummer has to use both hands. (This is not necessarily true with sequenced drum parts, although you may want to try to keep the feeling of something humanly playable.) The point of departure for the fill is important and must be based on the musical context and where the release comes in the other instruments. The fills below will get you started, but you must use your imagination and take your primary cues from the other parts in the overall musical arrangement. In general, short, simple statements will prove most effective in situations that call for fills.

*The Rhythm Book*

The following examples illustrate fills from both swing beats and shuffle beats, all employing eighth-note triplets. In the first example, the fill begins before the fourth beat, but the snare comes back in on beat 4 to create a normal-sounding backbeat. In the last example, the fill is created by layering first the hi-tom and then the low-tom with the snare drum.

# PART FOUR

# DRUM PROGRAMMING AND THE NEW TECHNOLOGY

# CHAPTER 14

# Drum Programming

The widespread availability and use of sequencers and drum and percussion samples has had a tremendous impact on the way popular music is being created, played, and recorded. These tools have generated completely new techniques for making drum rhythms. Today, the full range of drum sounds is at the fingertips of players, writers, and anyone else with an inclination to go out and lay down a couple of hundred dollars or less for a new musical toy. It's no longer necessary for a rhythm creator to be a drummer per se, although it's important for guitar players, keyboardists, composers, and arrangers who are doing serious drum programming to have a working knowledge of the traditional way rhythms blend with particular pop styles. This includes knowing how to construct drum rhythms and understanding the logic of contemporary drum patterns as constructed using sequencers, drum sound libraries, and samplers. So far in this book, we have explored this logic of drum rhythms extensively; in the following discussion, we'll take a look at some of the methods used to program basic drum rhythms.

## GETTING STARTED

The first order of business is to examine the basic procedures of programming using various simple rhythm figures. While this material is being presented with the assumption that you will be programming as you go along and using a sequencer as you follow the guidelines, it is not absolutely necessary that you do so. If you wish, you may read through this chapter quickly without immediately putting it into practice. However, this approach will not yield thorough understanding of the process, though it should provide a good basic idea of the way drum programming with sequencers is done and it will probably be sufficient for musicians who are not directly involved in the use of sequencers but wish to have a better understanding of this musical environment.

Sequencers generally employ two basic modes of programming. The first is *pattern* or *sequence* mode in which a short phrase is recorded into the sequencer's memory. These short patterns are the building blocks for the second mode of programming, called *song* or *composition* mode. In this mode, the shorter sequences are strung together into complete compositions.

Patterns of drum parts are normally created using one of two different techniques of programming: real-time or step-time. Initially you should try each process. Later you'll be stringing together short patterns to create a song or composition.

It's likely that some of the terminology used here will differ from that of your particular sequencers. But once the basic concepts are understood, the slight differences in terminology should be fairly easy to overcome. Sequencers that are part of dedicated work stations (synthesizers with sequencer functions) or sequencers (drum sample libraries with sequencer functions) will vary somewhat from the functioning of sequencers that are software programs for use on personal computers. Nonetheless, all of the following work should be easily accomplished on most any type of sequencer.

## STARTING A FILE

To get started, it is necessary to create a new file or select a new sequence. Almost all sequencers employ tracks as the basic building blocks, using the multitrack tape recorder as a model. Before recording any tracks, you must give the sequencer a basic musical framework. This means giving your sequences a time signature and a tempo. In this case set the time signature (or meter) to $\frac{4}{4}$ time and set the tempo, given in beats-per-minute, to 90 BPM.

## REAL-TIME PROGRAMMING

In real-time programming you actually play the rhythms into the sequencer by rhythmically pressing the individual keys on the keyboard (or buttons on a dedicated sequencer) as you listen to a metronome pulse playing at the tempo you have selected. The rhythms are recorded into the sequencer as you play them. This process can be repeated with a number of different sounds from the library of drum and percussion samples until you have a fully developed segment of rhythm. This technique resembles normal musical activity in that you actually create the rhythms in real time in relation to a pulse.

## SETTING THE VALUE OF THE CLICK AND COUNT-OFF

You must set the value of the metronome click that you will use to play your rhythms against. This may be automatically set (default) to a quarter note in your sequencer, but you may have the option of using a different note value for the click (though the $\frac{4}{4}$ time signature defines the beat as a quarter note). Generally, the quarter note will be the easiest beat to program with, though for complex rhythms it is sometimes easier to use an eighth-note click. For the rhythms we are currently programming, set the click to a quarter note.

On most sequencers you may also set the value of a count-off. This represents the number of bars that the metronome will play before the sequencer begins to record or play back. On some sequencers you may set the count-off to only occur during recording (this may be the default mode for count-off). This is generally the best mode because when playing back your sequence you do not need a count-off in order to prepare for recording. For these rhythms, set the count-off to one bar with the "count-off in record only" mode set.

Similarly, you may be able to set the click to only sound during recording. Again, this is generally the best mode because when playing back your sequence you do not need a click to perform a particular part. Of course, once some or all of your drum part has been programmed, you may want to disable the click and simply record to the existing tracks of your drum part. In this case you would want the "click in count-off only" mode so that you still have an audible count-off to get set to record. You should experiment with these various modes until you are comfortable using them.

## SEQUENCER VERSUS LOOP STYLE PROGRAMMING

When using the sequencer programming is generally accomplished by first selecting a number of bars for your pattern. This number of bars (say you select a one-bar pattern) is then looped during basic programming. This means that while you are recording a part there is one bar that is looped, and you may continue to record on that bar each time it comes around. This is particularly convenient for recording whole drum parts (e.g., kick drum, snare drum, hi-hat etc.) as the sequencer loops. This technique has its advantages in speed and simplicity but has significant disadvantages in overall flexibility. Standard sequencer style programming utilizes separate tracks for each drum element and acts as a continuous recorder, moving from one bar to the next until stopped. The advantage of having each of the parts of the drum pattern (e.g., kick drum, snare drum, hi-hat etc.) on an individual track is that it allows for greater ease and flexibility of editing. It also allows for different length loops within the same pattern (e.g,. the snare drum may be a one-bar loop, while the hi-hat is a four bar pattern that loops). Recording in sequence (as a opposed to loop style) recording also allows you to record a bunch of ideas and then go back and select what you like for use in your pattern. While most sequencers allow for drum machine–style recording, usually called loop recording, for our purposes we are going to employ the standard sequencer style programming in creating these drum patterns.

## INPUTTING A PATTERN IN REAL TIME

As an initial approach to programming, we'll consider two simple drum set rhythms. These are patterns based on the rock and pop beats discussed in Chapter Nine. We'll start with the following one bar pattern.

*Pattern 2*

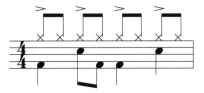

Start the sequencer in record mode set to record on an individual track. You should be hearing the metronome clicking in quarter notes. Usually the 1-beat is distinguished by a different sound or volume of click as the measure repeats around and around.

The ride pattern is more commonly played as a closed hi-hat sound than with an actual ride cymbal sound. The ride pattern in this beat is straight eighth notes, so tap the key assigned to the closed hi-hat as straight eighth notes, that is, two evenly spaced notes for each click of the metronome.

Next, place the hi-hat track into playback mode and go to a new track to program the kick drum part. Put this track into record and play the kick part shown in the above pattern by pressing the key assigned to a kick drum sound on the 1-beat, on the "and" of 2-beat, and on the 3-beat.

Now, place the kick drum track into playback mode and go to a new track to program the snare drum part. Put this track into record and play the snare part shown in the above pattern by pressing the key assigned to a snare drum sound on the 2-beat and on the 4-beat. Take that track out of record and play back your 1-bar drum pattern. (This is the opening drum part for the Beatles' song 'Sergeant Pepper's Lonely Heart's Club Band').

## QUANTIZING

Quantizing represents the most radically different musical capability that sequencers offer—and the general consensus is that it is both a blessing and a curse.

Quantizing represents the most radically different musical capability that sequencers offer—and the general consensus is that it is both a blessing and a curse. Quantizing means "correcting" the live rhythmic performance by moving all or some of the notes to the nearest perfectly accurate position. Say you set the quantizing function for a quarter-note value. This means that quarter notes are the smallest subdivisions of time available for the position of a note. This means that any note played will be "corrected" to sound on the nearest quarter note to the point when it was played. Thus, if you play a snare-drum beat (strike the snare button) between beats 2 and 3, when quantized that snare beat will be moved to whichever is the nearest of those two beats. Quantizing greatly simplifies the programming process because you don't have to perform the rhythm perfectly; you may approximate the performance and have the sequencer "correct" it to within the smallest note value you choose. You may also program part of a pattern and use one level of quantizing (say, eighth notes) and then switch the quantizing (to, say, sixteenth notes) when programming another part of the pattern.

Of course the blessing and the curse aspect of quantizing has to do with the meaning of "correct." Perfectly accurate performances are not necessarily desirable or musical. There have been many advancements in the subtle application of quantizing that have allowed the use of it to be much less regimented. For one thing, most programs now quantize in a nondestructive mode, which means that the original performance is not lost and can be returned to if desired. In the use of quantization, most computer-based programs allow for more subtle applications such as the degree of quantization—meaning that the programmer can determine the extent to which each note is corrected so that the performance is not made to be "perfect." One might move all notes 50 percent or 70 percent closer to their perfectly correct location. Many programs also allow the programmer to limit the notes that are quantized to those that are further away from a perfectly accurate location. Thus, only those notes that are inaccurate enough to sound "wrong" may be moved closer to their exact location—and again here, it may just be closer, not necessarily all the way to fully quantized location.

These advancements in quantizing have made the application of this process much more flexible. Nonetheless, it is interesting to note that the advent of drum programming and of quantization has led to an acceptance of perfectly quantized performances. While these were initially reviled by many (and still are by some), many popular genres have embraced the perfectly quantized sound of programmed drums—much of the dance music, hip-hop, and rap worlds commonly employ perfectly quantized performances, and not just in the drum parts. Even a fair amount of straight pop music and other contemporary genres find the use of perfectly quantized parts to be fairly common. This new technological capability represents a change in the ear of the Western popular music lover.

It is important to note that in fact all sequencers are quantizing to some degree at all times. This is because there is some level of resolution—usually 192 divisions per beat—that the sequencer must use to place notes. This is quite subtle—the movement of a note by one tick (that is one 192nd subdivision of a beat) is generally agreed to be inaudible and is useful information for when we develop some of the more subtle applications of rhythmic programming.

## COPY AND LOOP

Once you have established a basic drum beat for a song or composition, it is often easiest to develop and complete the drum program using a lot of copy and/or looping functions rather than reprogramming each section of the song from scratch. It is also usually best to create various sections of a song or composition as independent sequences which are then put together into a song form. We will discuss alternatives to this method when we look at putting whole songs together. Looping is a simple way of copying rhythms where sections are repeated by selecting the section to be looped and employing the looping function. Some sequencers only allow you to loop whole sequences, but most sequencers allow you to loop individual tracks independently. You may also usually set a limited number of loops or continuous looping. If we want to make our first drum track into an eight-bar rhythm, we could set each track to loop seven times. We could accomplish the same thing by copying each track and pasting it in sequence seven times. Many sequencers have a repeat function that allows you to copy a part of a track or sequence and repeat it a given number of times. This accomplishes the same thing as copying and pasting more quickly. Thus, by selecting the one-bar pattern we have created and repeating it seven times we create the same eight-bar rhythm we would have by individually pasting it seven times in sequence. Copying or repeating tracks to create song parts has the distinct advantage of allowing for changes in the rhythm, such as fills at the end of sections. Of course, you could simply loop the parts six times and then copy, paste, and edit the eighth bar to include a fill, but what if you want a small rhythm variation in bar four? By copying or repeating bars you give yourself easy access to editing and ultimately much more control over your composition than you have when looping.

After you have selected and repeated the one-bar patterns that you created to make Pattern 1, go back and select and copy the one-bar patterns again (all three tracks—kick, snare, and hi-hat). Start a new sequence or pattern within your file and paste these bars onto three new tracks. Use these to create the following new drum pattern shown.

*Pattern 2*

Note that Pattern 2 has the same hi-hat and snare patterns as Pattern 1, although they are written in a two-bar pattern. This is because the kick drum rhythm is two bars long. To make this new pattern from the copy of Pattern 1 you created, you must first edit the kick drum pattern into the new pattern shown above. This can be done by adding notes one at a time or by rerecording the kick track. Once that is done, simply repeat the one-bar hi-hat pattern seven times, repeat the one-bar snare pattern seven times, and repeat the two-bar kick pattern three times. You now have another eight-bar drum pattern. We will use these two patterns to make a song after we look at an alternate programming technique.

## STEP-TIME PROGRAMMING

With step-time programming, sequencers (and their more cumbersome predecessors) have introduced an entirely new technique for creating rhythms. Here rhythms are created out of the context of normal musical time. The sequencers are set to "step" through a pattern at a specific rate. For example, you can set a sequencer's metronome for a one-bar pattern and the stepping function at eighth notes. You may then "step through" the bar one eighth note at a time, advancing the pattern each time you enter an instrument sound or a rest. At each eighth-note location, you may add or delete any voice from the library of sounds by pressing the instrument key. Rhythms are then played back in time to the musical beat at the tempo you have set. Thus, you can create rhythms without any of the physical coordination of a drummer—without even coordinating the pressing of buttons in time to the beat. In fact, anyone can create complex or "unplayable" rhythms.

Real-time programming may also be combined with step-time programming in the creation of one pattern. It is often more efficient to input the simple parts of a pattern in real-time mode and then switch to step-time for loading a particularly tricky passage.

Once you are comfortable with creating patterns or sequences, you will want to create complete songs or compositions. Two different approaches may be taken. For an all-in-one–type approach, you may simply string patterns together, using the repeat and copy and paste functions to create one long sequence. You can usually place markers at various points to help keep track of where you are in the composition.

Another method of composing, which allows for easier reshuffling of parts and arrangements, involves song or compose mode on the sequencer. This mode allows us to string patterns together to create longer and more involved compositions or songs made up of separately created patterns. Although different sequencers use different ways to accomplishing this, the basic function is always the same: patterns are strung together to create whole new sequences.

Using insert, delete, and repeat allows you to construct and then edit the sequence of patterns that will make up the song structure. This process can become quite involved if the song you're working on contains many sections such as an introduction (intro), a verse, a chorus, a bridge, alternate verses, solos, vamps or "outros," and so on. Keeping in mind that verses, choruses, and other sections might eventually contain more than one drum pattern, you begin to see that a song may require a quite complicated rhythm part. However, the various sections are often closely related and may be relatively easy to program once the basic patterns have been created.

We have written two different patterns in the previous sections of this chapter; let's call Pattern 1 a verse pattern and Pattern 2 a chorus pattern. In song mode, you might string these patterns together into an alternating verse/chorus song form. Of course, most songs will require more patterns than these in order to create an appropriate drum part. Some songs, however, may use only one drum pattern through the entire song and really wouldn't require the use of song mode at all.

To make a more interesting drum program for your song, you may create many more patterns similar to Patterns 1 and 2 and string them together in song mode. These may be slightly different parts, completely different parts, or simply the same parts with different endings. A list of activities that would yield appropriate patterns might run something as follows:

• Start by renaming Pattern 1 "verse" and Pattern 2 "chorus."

• Create a new pattern for the intro. First take bar 1 of the verse pattern and copy it to a new sequence and call it "intro." Edit the intro by deleting the ride part and then entering a new ride pattern based on quarter notes. (You could also do this by clearing all of the "and" beats in the ride pattern.) Then add a bass drum beat on the "and" of 3. The resulting intro pattern should be as shown.

*Intro pattern*

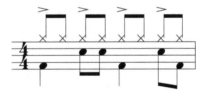

Repeat this bar three times in the intro sequence in order to create a four-bar intro.

• Create a new pattern for an alternate verse ending. Copy bar one of the verse pattern to new sequence and call it verse 2. Repeat this bar seven times in the new sequence in order to create an eight-bar alternate verse. Edit bar eight of this sequence by adding a kick drum beat to the "and" of 3 and a snare drum beat to the "and" of 4. These additional notes add a little more movement to the rhythm.

*Verse 2 ending*

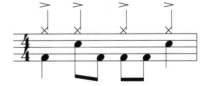

• Create an alternate chorus ending pattern by copying bars one and two of the chorus pattern and pasting them to a new sequence, and call it chorus 2. Repeat these two bars three times in the new sequence in order to create an eight-bar alternate chorus. Edit bar eight of this new sequence by adding snare drum beats on the "and" of beat 3 and the "and" of beat 4, and delete the kick drum beat from the "and" of 3. These additional snare notes add movement to the basic chorus pattern and are being used as a basic kind of fill.

*Chorus 2 ending*

• Create a bridge pattern from the existing chorus pattern by copying bars one and two of the chorus pattern and pasting them to a new sequence. Modify the kick drum part so that the kick plays only on beats 1 and 3 in both bars. Add a snare drum beat on the "and" of beat 2 in bar one and on both the "and" of beats 2 and 4 in bar 2. The new two bar pattern should be as follows:

*Bridge pattern*

Repeat these two bars three times in the new sequence in order to create an eight-bar pattern.

Let's say that the final song form is going to be as follows: intro, verse, verse, chorus, verse, chorus, double intro, bridge, chorus, chorus, chorus (assuming a fade at the end). The alternate endings you edited can be used to make the program more interesting and more natural-sounding. A final programmed song form that would employ these patterns, within the song structure outlined above, might use this following series of sequences: intro, verse, verse 2, chorus, verse 2, chorus, intro, intro, bridge, chorus 2, chorus 2, chorus 2. Lining the parts up with the arrangement gives a clearer picture of how you might use the new patterns and endings that you have created.

The ease of creating
slightly different
patterns for different
sections, different
endings for similar
sections, and whole new
arrangements by just
recombining sequences
makes song mode a very
powerful tool for the
composer/arranger.

| Arrangement | Patterns |
| --- | --- |
| Intro | Intro |
| Verse | Verse |
| Verse | Verse 2 |
| Chorus | Chorus |
| Verse | Verse 2 |
| Chorus | Chorus |
| Double Intro | Intro |
| | Intro |
| Bridge | Bridge |
| Chorus | Chorus 2 |
| Chorus | Chorus 2 |
| Chorus | Chorus 2 |

There are numerous choices for the location of these patterns, as well as many other related patterns and fills that you might have created and used. The ability to restructure the overall song form is an especially valuable tool for arranging. You can try different arrangements without losing the original by copying the song sequence to another song sequence and editing the newly created version into a different arrangement. The ease of creating slightly different patterns for different sections, different endings for similar sections, and whole new arrangements by just recombining sequences makes song mode a very powerful tool for the composer/arranger.

## OTHER FUNCTIONS

Sequencers provide numerous other functions beyond basic pattern and song programming. An important function for programming natural-sounding rhythms is accenting. Setting up different volume levels for different notes within a pattern can make otherwise mechanical sounding rhythms sound much more human.

Another available control that pertains to feel is known as the swing function, which allows you to place beats in other than the traditional musical locations (eighth notes, triplets, sixteenth notes, and so on). The swing function is really a form of quantizing, but the notes are placed in between normal values—between a proper eighth note and eighth-note triplet, for example. This function is in recognition of the fact that in natural human performance, notes are often intentionally displaced from their mathematically proper location in order to provide the rhythm with a looser feel. These and other more advanced programming functions will be discussed in a later chapter.

As you begin to work with sequencers, bear in mind that mastery comes only with a good deal of practice. Working back and forth between programming, listening, editing, and refining will eventually provide you with the skill necessary to begin programming complex rhythm parts without spending all day doing it. Try to avoid getting stuck in one method of programming. Use all the functions available to you, including both real- and step-time programming, various levels of quantization, and the copy and edit approaches to song building. Experiment with rhythms; bring your own judgment into play and get to the point where creating original rhythm parts on a sequencer becomes a natural and comfortable process.

# CHAPTER 15

# Advanced Programming

here is no substitute for repetition, whether you're practicing stick exercises on a drum or programming a sequencer rhythm. In order to program drum parts that sound like they might have been played by an actual drummer, you must combine advanced programming skills with knowledge of how a drummer plays. The goal is to eliminate the mechanical sound of strictly quantized drum parts—to bring musicality into the art of drum programming. There are two subtle ways of manipulating your rhythm programming so that this mechanical sound is replaced by more natural-sounding rhythms. The first of these is accenting; the second is shifting of time values.

## ACCENTING

**It is a lack of appropriate accenting that will most obviously distinguish programmed material from a live drummer.**

Interestingly, it is not the "perfect" time of strictly quantized rhythm parts that is primarily responsible for their mechanical sound. It is a lack of appropriate accenting that will most obviously distinguish programmed material from a live drummer. Sequencers provide accenting functions that can help to alleviate the stiff, mechanical feel. Numerous examples of accenting in pop rhythm can be found in the examples in Part Three. Here we look at the using those accenting options within sequenced parts.

When a drummer plays a drum set, the volume of each note of a performance will vary slightly. Similarly when programming a sequencer and using velocity sensitive keys, a different volume will register for each key stroke. Small variations in levels can create a very natural feel, even with mechanically perfect (quantized) time; however, inappropriate accenting in either amount or placement can make programmed material sound unnatural or wrong.

A simple example would be programming a basic eighth-note ride pattern. Were all the notes programmed to the same velocity (volume) this would sound very stiff (though appropriate to some contemporary idioms). The natural tendency of a drummer would be to play the quarter notes on the ride louder and the eighth notes in between quieter. Using the available 128 levels of volume used in MIDI, we might represent the eight eighth notes in one bar with the following eight volume levels: 125, 110, 125, 110, 125, 110, 125, 110. Here each quarter note has a volume of 125, with each intermediary eighth note a volume of 110. While this would sound more natural that a ride part where each note had the same value, it would still sound a little stiff. If we maintained this general approach but varied each note slightly, we would get an even more natural-sounding performance. Our MIDI volumes might read something like this: 127, 110, 123, 107, 125, 109, 124, 111. This begins to approach the natural variations that might occur if the part were played on a drum set.

In your experiments with accenting to obtain a natural feel, you might want to program some of the rhythms presented in Part Three. Although these examples show different levels of accenting, further variation of volume levels will provide even greater expression of the human element in drumming. Many sequencer programs have functions that will randomize velocity for you. Of course, unless you are entering parts with a keyboard that does not have velocity sensitivity or you have disabled this function, your performance will already contain a certain amount of volume variation. Depending on your ability to play parts with a drummer's feel, these volume variations may or may not be appropriate to a natural style. You may well need to go in and edit certain notes to bring them more in line with a natural drum performance. Generally, randomizing parts will create variation, but they may not be natural to performance. For example, randomizing volumes will never provide the kind of alternating accenting pattern just described for the ride part of a drum sequence. Playing parts in with the appropriate feel and then editing individual notes where necessary will generally provide the most natural sounding performances.

The computer's randomizing function may be valuable relative to certain repetitive drum parts such as backbeat snare drum hits. In this case, it is most natural sounding if all these beats are very similar in volume, though not identical. To use the randomizing function you might first program many bars of backbeat snare hits. There will be some natural variation in volume when you do this, and it may well be too much variation for the best sounding effect. If you randomize volumes at this point, you would be increasing the problem of too much variation in backbeat levels. You must first select all of the snare beats and set them to the same volume, say a MIDI velocity of 120. You would then employ the randomizing function using a small value for the function that limits how far in either direction the volume may be altered. If you selected two as the limit in both directions this would generate snare beats, in a random sequence, with volumes between 118 (two below) and 122 (two above). This kind of randomizing technique may approximate the performance of an outstanding studio drummer better than you are able to do with your own performance on a keyboard.

Further experimentation with variations of volume levels will provide even greater expression of the human element in drumming.

## SHIFTING TIME—SWING

The qualities which make some performers hotter or swing harder have been much debated and discussed. A certain consensus has developed that pertains to a particular kind of time shifting, and this function, often labeled swing, is provided on many sequencers.

The shifting of time values is another means of reducing mechanical feel, but it is more difficult to control or program. Its implementation in sequencers may take many forms but generally the most evolved one revolves around the swing function. The term *swing* isprimarily associated with jazz and has been used to describe a particular era in jazz history. The word has also been applied in a purely descriptive manner, as in the way we might characterize a band or a piece of music as "hot." The qualities which make some performers hotter or swing harder have been much debated and discussed. A certain consensus has developed that pertains to a particular kind of time shifting, and this function, often labeled swing, is provided on many sequencers. The traditional swing beat in jazz is expressed in the following ride pattern:

The two "ta" triplet beats (the "ta" of 2 and the "ta" of 4) create the skeleton of the triplet subdivisions that are prevalent in swing rhythms. It is through time shifting of these triplet embellishments that we express the swing function. The manipulation of swing has generally been thought of as the process of pushing the "ta" triplet beat closer to the following down beat. When done in extreme, the triplet may become an "a" sixteenth note instead. Thus the basic jazz rhythm is sometimes written (and sometimes played) as a sixteenth-note rhythm.

Even though this rhythm may be played as the ride pattern, the use of triplet subdivisions is most likely to occur in the rhythms of accompanying instruments. Interestingly, jazz rhythms are often written using straight eighth-note subdivisions, with the application of a "ta" triplet (or even an "a" sixteenth note) being assumed as the appropriate interpretation. Thus, the basic ride pattern may be written in eighth notes and played using either triplets or sixteenth notes.

These variations imply a flexible approach to the placement of the "ta" triplet, and this is what is at the heart of swing. The placement of the "ta" beat may be time-shifted so that it occurs anywhere in the space between a straight eighth note and a sixteenth note (or even closer to the following beat). Thus, the possible location of this swing beat embellishment may fall anywhere in the space shown.

On a sequencer, these swing beat variations are usually expressed in percentages. We program the beat as straight eighth notes and use the swing function to move the intermediary eighth note closer to the following down beats. Thus, a swing function of 50 percent maintains the straight eighth note (50 percent is halfway between the two downbeats, thus equal to a straight eighth note). A swing function of 67 percent (technically 66 2/3 percent) would be equal to the true "ta" triplet, as this is two-thirds of the way from one downbeat to the next. At 75 percent, the straight eighth note has become a true sixteenth note.

The swing function usually provides additional options between a straight eighth note and a "ta" triplet through entering a percentage that isn't one of these standard musical amounts—say 58 percent . A percentage such as this creates notes that cannot be expressed using the standard notation system (unless extremely small note values are used), and they allow a greater degree of expression in the rhythms you create. When the "ta" triplet is moved closer to the following downbeat, a tighter, bouncier, more hard-swinging feel is created. When the "ta" triplet is held back closer to the preceding eighth note, a more relaxed, looser feel is created. The ability of musicians and programmers to adjust rhythms in this way is a central part of expressing feeling in music.

While the swing function relates to the placement of what are essentially embellishment notes, or subdivisions of the main beat, the placement of actual beats may also be manipulated using time shifting. In basic rock and pop, this will mostly happen on the snare drum backbeats (beats 2 and 4). The kick drum beats on 1 and 3 become the control beats that define the mathematical time. The 2 and 4 beats may then be moved either in front of the beat or behind the beat. In front of the beat (sometimes referred to as "on top of the beat") means the snare actually plays before the mathematically correct 2- or 4-beat; behind the beat places the snare just past the mathematically correct locations. Generally before the beat creates a more driving kind of feel, behind the beat provides a heavier, more "grooving" kind of feel.

> **Time-shifting effects must be created using very small movements or they will simply sound like errors.**

Time-shifting effects must be created using very small movements or they will simply sound like errors. Variations of this kind are better expressed in the smallest increments of time on a sequencer (often call "ticks") than in note values, because the note values would have to be so small to be usable (when do you really deal with a 256th note?). Many sequencers provide 480 ticks to each quarter note beat (240 ticks to an eighth note, etc.). This means that the exact length of a tick depends on the tempo (one tick at 60 BPM is twice as long as one tick at 120 BPM.)

Consistently placing the snare drum two to four ticks either in front of or behind the beat may produce a natural feel (from more "grooving" or "in the pocket" to more "driving" or "snappy"). More than this (depending on the tempo) may feel like rushing if before the beat and dragging if behind the beat. Randomizing functions may help to produce these effects. Some sequencers allow for randomized beat placement with control over degree of randomization as well as selection for placement only before, only after, or before and after the mathematically correct beat placement.

There are other interesting aspects of time shifting. Notes placed behind the beat will tend to be less insistent, and complex parts may serve a more natural, less disruptive function when played or programmed in this way. On the other hand, notes before the beat will push harder and call attention to themselves, perhaps providing a needed lift to a particular phrase. Drum fills, often used to move the music from one section to the next, may suggest the direction of movement by being slightly behind the beat when moving to a quieter passage or slightly ahead of the beat when going to a more driving section. This brings up the question of using time shifting consistently through various sections of a song or composition. Sometimes it is effective to approach each section differently. You may lay back on the verse and then push the chorus, for example.

**Musicians have always incorporated time shifting into their playing, consciously or not. Technology is providing the tools that allow this kind of extensive subtlety in programming.**

Sequencing of instruments other than drums may also contribute to a much more natural-sounding feel in programmed music. Musicians have always incorporated time shifting into their playing, consciously or not. Technology is providing the tools that allow this kind of extensive subtlety in programming. It is also providing the means to quantify information from human performances. We are now able to measure and analyze the exact amount of time shifting employed by a performer in a given performance. When this is done, a kind of map is created showing the position, relative to the beat, of each note played. This map can be used to drive the rhythms of a sequencer program, effectively (though not necessarily appropriately) translating the feel. This is an area that will continue to develop—many sequencers come with groove templates that may employ time shifting. Conversely, we have already seen that some popular music purposely uses strictly quantized drum parts as part of the sound of the idiom.

## IMITATIVE VERSUS NONIMITATIVE APPROACH

When programming rhythms with a sequencer, the user has a choice to make: whether to consistently try to create patterns that are playable by a real drummer, or whether to ignore real life playability and instead generate rhythms that are possible only when programmed. There are many limitations to the rhythms a drummer can play on the drum set, partly due to the drummer's limited number of limbs. When a drummer plays a tom-tom fill, for example, he or she must naturally stop the hi-hat pattern in order to free the hands for the fill. When you program with a sequencer, the hi-hat pattern may continue to play during the fill. If you stop the hi-hat pattern for the fill, you are using an imitative approach, programming what would be natural and necessary for the drummer. If you allow the hi-hat to continue to play during the fill, you are using a nonimitative approach.

> **There is no right or wrong answer to whether an imitative or nonimitative approach should be used, but you should be aware of the differences and apply whichever approach sounds and feels the best to you.**

The question of imitative versus nonimitative arises when you are programming drum fills, but it is also a general issue in the creation of complex rhythms that may be technically impossible to play but can still be programmed on with sequencers. There is no right or wrong answer to whether an imitative or nonimitative approach should be used, but you should be aware of the differences and apply whichever approach sounds and feels the best to you.

It is not only in programming that "impossible" drum parts can be created. Today's recording techniques allow drummers to play parts that would be impossible to play all at one time. For example, studio drummers may use the nonimitative approach to drum fills by overdubbing parts after the original rhythms have been recorded. As more and more different techniques come into widespread usage, this distinction becomes less and less significant. The listener has come to accept a wide variety of rhythmic approaches regardless of their relationship to the natural approach of a single trap drummer

# Electronic Drums

**Increased computer power has allowed for considerable advancements in the degree to which contemporary electronic drum sets can mirror acoustic drum performance.**

**U**p to this point, our discussion of the new wave of electronic instruments has focused on drum and percussion programming. The electronic drum set that is actually played rather than programmed is also an important part of the technological music environment. These sets generally consist of a group of drum pads set up in a typical drum set configuration that are played with regular drum sticks. They usually include a pad that is triggered with a standard (or slightly modified) bass drum pedal as well as a hi-hat pad linked to its own pedal. Increased computer power has allowed for considerable advancements in the degree to which contemporary electronic drum sets can mirror acoustic drum performance.

## ELECTRONIC DRUM SETS

Electronic drum sets that are actually played rather than programmed have become a common replacement for, or addition to, the traditional drum set. Electronic drum kits normally consist of drum pads which can be struck with a stick like an acoustic drum. The pad itself makes almost no sound, but it triggers a sound which is produced by a module linked to the pad. The sound module or "brain" usually consists of a variety of drum sounds similar to those in a sampler or a work station's drum sound library, along with various other percussion voices. The drum pads use small microphones within the pads to sense the striking of the stick and to translate that into an electronic pulse used to trigger a drum or percussion sound. Some of these drum pads are simple MIDI triggers that may be used to trigger any sound from a standard sound module. In its most basic operational mode, the musician strikes the pad with a drum stick and this triggers a digital sample of the desired drum or percussion sound. Most of the electronic drum sets also include sound modules with a variety of features that go far beyond the capabilities of a standard bank of digitally sampled drum and percussion sounds.

Prior to the use of digitally recorded drum sounds, the sounds of an electronic drum were synthesized using analog technology. Analog sounds start with a tone generator and simulate drum sounds by manipulating a simple tone. Tones are created using different kinds of sound waves, which produce different qualities of sound (timbres). Other kinds of sounds, such as white noise (a combination of all the frequencies) may also be mixed with the tones. The basic characteristics of the tone are manipulated by altering what is called the *envelope* of the tone. The envelope includes the relative volume and duration of the attack, sustain, decay, and release (ASDS) of the tone. The pitch of the tone may also be altered while retaining the basic timbre of one instrument. By altering only the pitch, for example, it is possible to simulate various sized tom-toms from one tom-tom sound.

Analog drum sounds tend to have a characteristic "electronic" timbre which is identifiable as synthetic. The classic Roland TR808 and TR909 drum machines used these analog-based drum sounds. When digitally sampled drum sounds, with their vastly more accurate reproduction of actual drum sounds, became available, these analog sounds were largely abandoned. They have since been rediscovered as classic electronic drum sounds and have become quite popular, especially with rap and hip-hop artists. They are now commonly found along with digitally sampled recordings of drums in many electronic drum modules and samplers. Ironically, these analog drum simulations now generally consist of digital samples of original analog sounds so that they can be used within the basic sample playback environment.

For the purposes of our discussion here, we will use the new Roland TD-40 V-drums as the primary model for electronic drums. This will allow us to touch on the basics of electronic drums and discuss the advancements that have been made, as the V-drums represent the most advanced version of electronic drums currently on the market.

*Roland TD-40 V-drums*

## DRUM PADS

The basic electronic drum pad features a rubber surface similar to the kind of practice pad that drummers have used for decades. These pads have a response similar to a normal drum head but make very little noise when struck. The V-drums also employ floating nylon heads, which are even more true to the feel of acoustic drums but also produce very little sound themselves. The microphone sensor translates the impact of the drum stick into an electronic pulse that is used to trigger the sound. At the very least, this system allows for velocity sensitivity, which may be translated into volume dynamics—when the pad is struck lightly, the drum sample is triggered at a low volume; when struck firmly, the volume is loud. The velocity sensitivity may be variable (user-selectable) and the degree of variation in volume usually corresponds to the 127 steps in the MIDI standard.

> The sound of drums will change relative to pitch, tambre and decay depending on where and how they are struck.

Of course, variations in volume are only one element in the characteristics of a drummer's performance when playing on acoustic drums. The sound of drums will change relative to pitch, tambre and decay depending on where and how they are struck. In early drum machine modules, Roland (R-8 and R-8M) added an element of pitch shifting that was dependent on velocity—different velocities would produce small shifts in pitch for the same drum sample. This helps to produce a more realistic acoustic drum simulation. With the V-drum, Roland has incorporated more of the tambre and decay characteristics to the drum sounds. In order to do this, the traditional sample playback technique of reproduction was abandoned for a more advanced sound-modeling technique. This is combined with sophisticated microphone-sensing techniques within each pad that allow the V-drums to alter sounds based on where they are struck on the pad—they call this *positional sensing*. The sound of a drum or cymbal will alter dramatically depending on where it is struck. The resonance of a drum will increase as you get closer to the center (though there is a dead spot at dead center) and the resonance of a cymbal will increase as you get closer to the edge. The resonance of the instrument effects pitch, tambre, and decay. Some of the sounds in the V-drum module are basic sampled sounds, but the modeled sounds allow this positional sensing within the pad to dictate variations in resonance that add a very sophisticated and realistic sound to the V-drums.

> The resonance of a drum will increase as you get closer to the center (though there is a dead spot at dead center) and the resonance of a cymbal will increase as you get closer to the edge. The resonance of the instrument effects pitch, tambre, and decay.

Most electronic drum sets use a combination pedal and pad to simulate the playing of a standard hi-hat. Just as with an acoustic hi-hat, the drummer is able to control the opening and closing of the cymbals with the pedal while playing the hi-hat sound with a drumstick on the pad. The V-drums add a hi-hat model that allows for the change in cymbal decay that occurs on a closed hi-hat depending on how close to the edge it is struck—closer to the edge produces more decay. All electronic drums provide a cross-sticking option for the sound of the snare drum (often, though mistakenly, referred to as "rim"—this is the sound made when the stick is held to one side of the drum rim and used to strike the other side of the rim, without ever hitting the drum head). The V-drums positional sensor allows a single pad to recognize the cross-sticking position and to differentiate this from the striking of the pad head. Again, this provides a more accurate representation of acoustic drum performance. Finally, the V-drum has added to the pad technology by giving it the capability of "choking" a cymbal. By grabbing the pad, the drummer is able to stop the ringing of a cymbal, effectively choking the sound off in the same way one would when grabbing an acoustic cymbal.

## SOUND MODULE

Although most of the sound modules provide a large number of sounds, there are usually some expansion capabilities for adding more sounds.

The sound module that comes with an electronic drum set typically has many standard drum and percussion sounds available as digital samples. Different sounds can be assigned to any of the drum pads to allow for configurations that include standard drum sets as well as access to more exotic set-ups that feature percussion and/or sound effects. Many preset drum kits, drum and percussion ensembles, or other pad and sample arrangements are provided, along with a number of user storable configurations. There are trigger inputs available for each pad separately, generally between eight and twelve, as well as individual outputs and a master stereo output. The trigger inputs have control over sensitivity so that the overall response of the drum pad is controllable. This kind of trigger input may also be used for other input sources such as triggering from mics used with acoustic drums or directly from prerecorded drums off of tape.

The sound module will generally include a variety of mixer functions that provide individual volume settings for the independent outputs as well as panning control. The mixer section may also allow for reassignment of the individual trigger inputs to either specific trigger outputs and/or the master stereo output. There may be EQ control as well; the V-drum features two-band fully parametric EQ on each individual output as well as global three-band EQ on the master stereo output. The mixer section may also include effects sends, and the unit is likely to have at least one on-board effects processor. This allows for the addition of reverb and/or delay effects that are individually controllable for each sound.

Although most of the sound modules provide a large number of sounds, there are usually some expansion capabilities for adding more sounds. These may be stock sound libraries from the manufacturer or specialty libraries from third-party providers. Some electronic kits provide user sampling capabilities, that is, the ability to record a particular drum, percussion instrument, trash can lid, or dog barking, and then use that as a sound to be programmed to trigger from one of the pads.

> For the home studio that wants to break out of the limitations of sequenced drum parts but is unable to record acoustic drums because of space limitations, volume problems, and/or equipment limitations, the new generation of electronic drums are particularly appealing.

The sound modules also provide MIDI implementation along with at least rudimental sequencing functions. This means that the module can be accessed from other sources such as keyboard controllers. The sequencer will provide at least "scratch pad" capabilities so that the user can record, play back, and store pad performances. Although the editing functions of the on-board sequencer may be minimal, the MIDI capabilities allow performances to be stored to external sequencers, which will allow for much greater editing flexibility. In this way, the performer may record performances that are combined with other MIDI and acoustic recordings. The performances may then also be used to trigger sounds from modules other than the module that is provided with the electronic drums. These kind of combinations of performances will be discussed more fully in the following chapter.

The V-drum sounds that use the sound modeling architecture provide many advancements in the ability to select and alter the qualities of the drums and their environment. Each instrument may be altered in regards to the depth of the drum, the type of drum shell , the drum head type, and the muffler type. This provides a boggling array of options and, on top of this, numerous environment and recording options are provided. These include the room size and wall material (e.g., a large wood room or a small tile room) as well as mic position. There are also ambience options in addition to the ambience provided by the on-board effects processor. Some of the options are subtle and some dramatic, but in total they provide dramatically expanded possibilities in the variations and flexibility of drum sounds.

## USES OF ELECTRONIC DRUMS

Electronic drums have found acceptance in a wide variety of situations. The traditional advantages of electronic drums over acoustic drums are the ability to control volume level and the ability to edit performances. The latest advancements in this technology, as indicated by the features of the V-drums, has broadened the appeal of electronic drums beyond these fundamentals.

On the most basic level, the ability for a drummer to practice without disturbing the neighbors (or the whole neighborhood for that matter) gave the electronic drums their initial entrance into the marketplace. The advent of home recording and project studios, along with the advancements in the electronic drums themselves, have expanded the usefulness of these drums considerably. Of course, volume is often a concern for the home recordist as well. Add to this the ability to edit performances and, now, the ability to simulate an astounding array of sounds and sonic qualities, and the electronic drums have an even greater usefulness. For the home studio that wants to break out of the limitations of sequenced drum parts but is unable to record acoustic drums because of space limitations, volume problems, and/or equipment limitations, the new generation of electronic drums are particularly appealing.

**Nonetheless, despite all of the latest innovations, acoustic drums still provide the greatest degree of subtlety of expression and continue to be the preferred instrument for most of the world's drummers.**

For the performing drummer, the appeal of electronic drums still includes the ever-present volume issue. In small club type situations, electronic drums are a means of controlling volume —even if a drummer is capable of controlling their own volume, the fact is that drums don't sound the same when they are played softly. Electronic drums provide access to big drum sounds at low levels. They also allow for access to a much wider variety of sounds than a drummer is able to coax out of an acoustic set and provide the performing drummer the stability of a consistent sound, where variations in microphones, room acoustics, and mixing engineers may be more likely to compromise the sound of acoustic drums. Of course, some of these factors may also compromise the sound of electronic drums, but they are less likely to do so to the same extent. Nonetheless, despite all of the latest innovations, acoustic drums still provide the greatest degree of subtlety of expression and continue to be the preferred instrument for most of the world's drummers.

# CHAPTER 17

# Sampling, Looping, and Composite Rhythms

**By combining many different ways of constructing rhythms and manipulating sounds, whole new possibilities for creating grooves have emerged.**

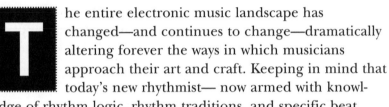he entire electronic music landscape has changed—and continues to change—dramatically altering forever the ways in which musicians approach their art and craft. Keeping in mind that today's new rhythmist— now armed with knowledge of rhythm logic, rhythm traditions, and specific beat patterns for particular grooves—is best advised to keep up with the latest developments or be left stranded in the rapidly dissipating dust of low tech, we now embark on an inbound tour through the heartland of the new musical technoscape.

Along with the new technological tools, entirely new methods of composing and arranging have emerged, which also employ a greatly expanded rhythmic vocabulary. These new tools have emerged from the evolution of digital sound manipulation. They combine a variety of digital technologies that have been with us for some time but are only now being made accessible together in one piece of hardware or through one software program. By combining many different ways of constructing rhythms and manipulating sounds, whole new possibilities for creating grooves have emerged. The following discussion explores these provocative new technologies.

## ELEMENTS OF THE NEW STYLE

The rhythmic evolution of electronic music started with a behemoth known as an arpeggiator. Combined with the early electronic sound generating devices, these arpeggiators created very simple repeating rhythms. The concept was rudimental—sixteen consecutive steps that each triggered an electronic sound. The speed of the steps, as well as the pitch and tambre of the sound, could be manipulated so that repeating phrases could be generated—an electronically created arpeggio. The concept was as old as music itself, but the implementation was completely cutting edge. The results were musically very fundamental, but the sounds produced had never been heard before. The arpeggios were not new in musical terms and were very basic in musical concept, but they suggested two important developments in the ability to create music. The first was the ability to program rhythms out of time and then play them back using electronic technology—a means of rhythmic creation that offered a world of potential that was entirely new. Until then, rhythms had to be played to be heard. The second was rhythmically "perfect" performances. The electronic generation of rhythm allowed for purely metronomic accuracy in the performance of musical rhythms. This was an aspect of electronic music that had been derided for decades. However, while programming features slowly became powerful enough to create subtle, human inconsistencies to programmed rhythmic performances, over the same period of time rhythmically "perfect" sounding tracks have become accepted by large numbers of musicians and audiences of many popular musical styles.

The idea of sequencers developed from these early arpeggiators and took hold in the form of drum machines—rudimental electronic "recorders" with a library of analog percussion sounds that allowed for the programming of basic drum parts. These early drum machines provided arpeggiator style sequencing in that they allowed for a certain number of steps (usually sixteen) that could be programmed with various percussion sounds or as rests. A very limited number of sounds were available and only the most basic kinds of rhythms could be programmed, yet the very idea of programming music opened up a world of new possibilities for musicians and began the technological revolution which has become such a major part of music making today.

Two contemporary products that harken back to these original concepts are E-mu's Audity 2000 and Steinberg/Propellerhead's Rebirth. The Audity 2000 is a synthesizer module that includes sixteen simultaneous arpeggiators. This synth is entirely tempo-based in operation and also includes a sound set of modern drum kits, industrial noise type sound effects, and sampled analog waveforms that recall the analog sounds found on those early arpeggiators. There are also numerous clock-based modulation sources that, together with the arpeggiators, allow for the creation of very complex and modern style sequences.

Rebirth is a software program and, as the name implies, it is the revival of some previous technology—in this case the early drum machine and bassline sequencers that were made by Roland Corp. The software reproduces the 808 and 909 drum machines, along with two 303 bass sequencers, and simply stacks the interfaces together onto one computer screen.

*Propellerhead's Rebirth program*

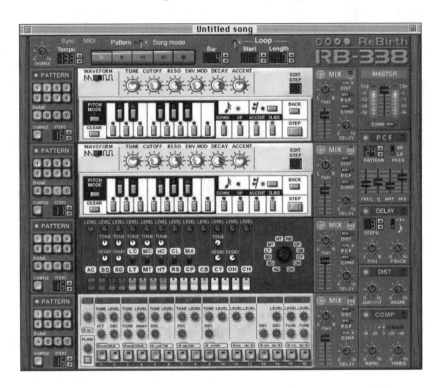

These were the first of the programmable drum machines that were available at an affordable price, and they were very popular. The addition of the bassline sequencers allowed for complete, if very rudimental, programmed rhythm sections. Rebirth does a great job of reproducing all of the features of these now "classic" machines and adds a variety of new features without compromising the basic sound or feel of the originals. The program also offers an arpeggiator to complete the set of "antique" programming features.

While these early forms of technologically based music making were revolutionary in themselves, the true revolution didn't really get going until we moved from these analog-based machines into the digital world. The great leap forward came with the acceptance of the MIDI (musical instrument digital interface) standard. MIDI allowed for true compatability for all digitally based sequencers and synthesizers. On the sequencer side, this led to computer-based sequencers that have evolved, along with personal computers, into highly sophisticated tools for the recording and manipulation of musical performances via MIDI data.

The other side of the digital revolution came in the form of digital recording. It began with simple digital samples that were much more accurate representations of things such as drums than anything analog synthesis could produce—this, of course, was because they were actual digital recordings of drums rather than electronic simulations. The combination of MIDI sequencers with digital drum samples produced the ability to create very realistic sounding drum parts with a high degree of control, including that formerly illusive ability to create music outside of musical time, "programming" music.

Digital recording gave birth to a whole new breed of music instrument known as samplers. As the name suggests, samplers use digital recordings (or samples) of musical instruments (or other sounds) to provide digital representations of all different kinds of sounds. The digital nature of these recordings means that they can be manipulated in many ways that were previously unavailable in the analog realm, and the devices can be controlled using the MIDI protocol for sequencing. While digital samples of drums represents a pretty straightforward use of this technology, this gets somewhat more complicated in dealing with sampled versions of tonal musical instruments. Instruments that have tremendous variation in both pitch and sustain provide a much greater challenge for a sampler. Because of the relative expense of digital memory (especially when samplers first began to appear), it was necessary to find ways to provide the full range of musical pitches and the ability to have a note that could sustain for a long time (at least equivalent to the natural sustain of the instrument that was sampled) using the least possible memory. Pitch was dealt with by taking samples at various intervals and filling the intermediary pitches by interpolation; sustain was dealt with using the art of looping. Looping in this instance means taking a short sample of the instrument and looping that same sample to provide continuous sustain. In this way, samplers are used to simulate acoustic music instrument performances with reasonable demands on digital memory storage.

Of course, digital memory has become much cheaper, and samplers have evolved to become much more sophisticated tools. Some modern sample playback instruments have several long samples of every note of an acoustic piano to reproduce

...looping of digital recordings has progressed far beyond being used just to provide musical sustain while conserving digital memory and has taken on a whole new meaning and purpose in the creation of contemporary music.

not only each note's tambre, but the tambre of that note when played at soft, medium, or loud volumes. In the meantime, the looping of digital recordings has progressed far beyond being used just to provide musical sustain while conserving digital memory and has taken on a whole new meaning and purpose in the creation of contemporary music.

## RHYTHM LOOPING AND MODERN MUSIC MAKING

Using loops of full rhythmic phrases started with the appropriation of samples (digital recordings) from existing, often classic, pop recordings of the past. It began in the rap/hip-hop world and generally consisted of one or two bar phrases of drum or drum and bass passages from famous R&B tunes. These phrases would be used as underpinnings of entirely new compositions that were composed over the looped phrases. While credit and compensation issues raged, the practice did not diminish but rather expanded into other related areas. Today, along with loops from classic (or obscure) recordings by other artists (including contemporary as well as classic recordings), looping also draws from a vast library of original "loop-ready" recordings that are released from copyright requirements by the simple purchase of the CD or other software package. While drum loops still dominate in this world, there are loops of all different kinds of musical phrases and instrumentation in use. Many of the CD or software packages are optimized for use in popular samplers. And rhythmical looping is no longer the sole domain of the rap/hip-hop world but has permeated virtually every style of popular music production.

There are many software programs that focus on looping capabilities or looped phrases. The program Peak from Berkley Integrated Audio Software (BIAS) is a two-channel digital audio editing program that features sophisticated tools to be used in the creation of loops, along with a myriad of other editing functions. Unlike previous editors, Peak incorporates time-based (tempo and meter) considerations in helping the user find the optimal loop points in a sample. The program will point the user to the right region for looping if given the tempo and meter of the phrase. Peak also provides the ability to fine-tune the loop point by showing a close-up view that can be adjusted while listening to the transition. It also provides cross-fading functions that assist in any kind of digital editing process. These specialized looping functions may be used in the creating of rhythm loops, such as the drum phrases discussed here, or in the creation of musical instrument loops that can provide the kind of sustain function needed for acoustic instrument recreations. These added looping functions within the domain of a standard two-channel editor reflect the importance of loop creation in current musical styles.

On the other end of the looping spectrum is the software program GrooveMaker from IK Multimedia. This is not a tool for loop creation but rather a kind of music making playground that builds grooves from loops that already exist. The loops come grouped together in a what is called a song. The loops within a song all share the same tempo and musical key, so they will all play together musically in any combination. The user can select up to eight different loops from a selection of over 60 different loops which are grouped according to categories such as percussion, fx, melody lines, etc. When a song is selected, a default groove with six tracks comes up in the groove window, but editing is very simple. Loops can be selected for any of the eight tracks and then tracks can be soloed or muted, and their volume and panning relationship can be changed.

With so many loops to choose from and with control of volume and panning, a huge number of very different grooves can be created from any one song. Tempo is also controllable by either switching BPM (beats per minute) or by tap tempo. Tap tempo allows you to select the tempo by tapping the mouse clicks in rhythm. The program determines the tempo of the mouse clicks and resets the tempo of the groove to coincide with it. This kind of tap tempo function has become very popular on all hardware and software tools that are rhythm based and is a very convenient way of controlling tempo. It is especially useful in live situations where DJs or performers wish to synchronize grooves. In GrooveMaker, a variety of other default grooves can be selected for use or as starting points for editing. This program is very intuitive and fun for a complete novice as well as useful for the professional, especially one involved in the highly loop-oriented areas of music such as dance or hip-hop.

*IK Multimedia's Groovemaker program*

GrooveMaker also contains an arpeggiator that provides a whole secondary music creating tool. The arpeggiator is kind of a virtual synth that comes with a wide variety of synthesizer sounds. Arpeggios are created by clicking notes on the music keyboard icon. In keeping with the user-friendly approach, GrooveMaker will even highlight the notes on the synth that will harmonize with the key of the current song. GrooveMaker also contains a "remix" page which allows the user to string saved grooves together, and a DJ Remix page, which is sort of a random remixer function that operates in various musical styles. GrooveMaker has a lot of musical power, but it is also fun and easy to use. It can be used to just groove along with, in more serious applications such as the creation of soundtrack material, or even as a tool in live performances.

## THE WHOLE KIT AND CABOODLE

At the forefront of today's rhythm making revolution are software and hardware products that provide many functions relating to the creation of grooves all in one package. These generally include sampling capabilities oriented toward phrase looping as well as sequencer capabilities. They will often include sound libraries of both phrases and individual sounds for looping or sequencing. They provide mixing functions so that at a minimum the volume and panning of multiple sound sources is controllable. Generally these units will also allow for altering the tempo of phrases without changing the pitch, taking advantage of the particular nature of digital audio. And, in line with their fundamental digital nature, they generally provide an effects processor or two (i.e., a DSP—digital signal processor) to manipulate the sound with.

One such box is the Zoom SampleTrak. At the heart of the SampleTrak is the ability to play multiple phrases using the unit's drum machine–like pads to trigger the start of the phrase. SampleTrak comes with a large library of sounds and phrases but can also sample phrases from virtually any source. It also includes an on-board sequencer that gives it more traditional drum machine type capabilities, and it does have MIDI implementation. A play list function allows you to assemble parts into a song structure. The pad triggers give the user a lot of real time control that makes the unit especially useful for live performance. An extensive effects processor allows for simple or radical alteration of the samples. Along with basic DSP functions such as chorus or delay, the effects processor adds more disruptive type processing such as "Extreme EQ" or "Lo-Fi." These effects can alter samples into completely unrecognizable versions of the original, though they generally maintain the same basic rhythmic qualities (tempo and meter). Layering loops with varied effects provides the basis for some of the most original-sounding grooves in the modern music vocabulary.

*The Zoom SampleTrak*

SampleTrak also provides the ability to match tempos of different samples without changing pitch. It does this by digitally resampling the phrase to fit into an assigned amount of time. As long as the phrases are set to loop in a rhythmic fashion, once they fit into the same amount of time they will play in tempo together. As we shall see, other units deal with this issue of synchronizing sampled phrases in different ways.

On the software side, the most influential loop-based program is ACID from Sonic Foundry. This program has succeeded in making what used to be very complicated multiple looping procedures quite simple. The key is a proprietary coding system that encodes tempo and pitch information in a format that allows for automatic matching of loop tempos and keys. ACID provides a kind of digital multitracking format for virtually any number of tracks (based on system RAM) to be assembled from the large library of loops. Because of the encoding system, loops that are brought into a session are automatically set to play in time and pitch together. Using this same system, tempos and pitches of loops can be changed together in real time. ACID also provides extensive effects processing capabilities through the now familiar plug-in implementation, as well as basic volume and panning mix functions. ACID does not have MIDI implementation but it does have automation available for the mix and effects functions and it can be synced to other units (such as ADATS or other tape machines) using MIDI Time Code/SMPTE. These functions all make ACID somewhat similar to a multitrack digital audio program, though it's really stripped down to the tools necessary for working with loops that makes it very simple to use. The automatic tempo and pitch matching function adds an ease of use which truly makes ACID a breakthrough product.

*Sonic Foundry's ACID program*

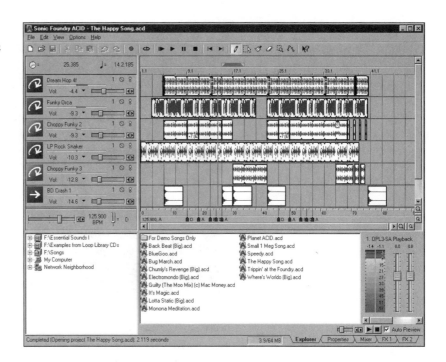

Similar to ACID on the hardware side is Yamaha's Loop Factory (SU700). The Loop Factory incorporates "intelligent rhythm matching" without the need for proprietary file formats like ACID uses. Instead, the Loop Factory slices or "atomizes" the sample into small segments, based on amplitude characteristics. In this way, a loop is broken into pieces, making it more like a MIDI file that is composed of a lot of separate drum elements made up of individual samples. Not only can the tempo of the loop be easily altered without changing pitch, but, the loop can be edited like a MIDI file, adding or deleting elements and even quantizing. Like a similar piece of software from Steinberg/Propellerhead called Recycle, which exports these processed loops to a sampler or audio-capable sequencer to be used in conjunction with sequenced files, the Loop Factory has an on-board sequencer for standard sequencing functions. It also has traditional drum machine–type pads (like Zoom's SampleTrak) and the Loop Factory adds a "scratch" pad (ribbon controller) that can be used for DJ-type scratching effects. These controllers help make the Loop Factory valuable for live performance. Along with its sampling capabilities, the Loop Factory incorporates mixer functions for all the various sampled or programmed tracks. As with ACID, many of the mix functions have automation, and there is extensive effects processing available for all tracks.

*Yamaha's Loop Factory (SU700)*

There are many other similar products by all of the major manufacturers of professional audio tools and software developers. They incorporate various combinations of the elements that we've seen here. By the time you read this, there will be new features within whole new related products. There is no doubt that these hybrid machines and software engines that incorporate many elements in the digital lexicon of audio composing, recording, editing, processing, and playback will continue to pave the way to the future of music making.

## PAST, PRESENT, FUTURE

The past, present, and future of music making merge into a continuous stream of creative endeavors. However, the application of highly sophisticated audio software for computers and equally sophisticated digitally based sound modules has added new dimensions to the process of creating music. Just the practice of programming musical performances outside of musical time represents an unheard of capability until as recently as a few decades past. The ability to digitally translate, analyze, and manipulate timing and dynamic factors in rhythm performances opens up vast new areas of music production. However, people have been composing music for centuries and the intricacies of performance have been analyzed and manipulated by musicians for equally as long with great subtlety and vision, if with much less sophisticated tools.

The ability to digitally translate, analyze, and manipulate timing and dynamic factors in rhythm performances opens up vast new areas of music production. However, people have been composing music for centuries and the intricacies of performance have been analyzed and manipulated by musicians for equally as long with great subtlety and vision, if with much less sophisticated tools.

This marriage of recording and sound processing techniques with musical performance information, all expressed as digital data, does set the mind reeling with its creative potential. It also leaves the mind a bit stunned with the load of technical information necessary to function in the current musical environment. Fortunately, you needn't know every twist and turn of the digital landscape, just as you needn't know every musical style or concept. A balanced base of knowledge for today's musician, however, includes drum beats, MIDI, sequencers, and basic recording technology, as well as music fundamentals such as notation.

The creative process is constantly changing as both the technology and the people who use it grow and develop. Stripped to its fundamental, however, music recording may be traced back from hard disk recorders to analog multitrack systems to the beginning of sound reproduction to the system of notation to the aural tradition to speech itself and, finally, to the basics of communication. Rhythm, as we have already found, is as natural to human beings as speech. Music is a fundamental means of human communication. Digital creation and manipulation of music is simply an extension of this most primitive of man's capabilities. And though technology will undoubtedly continue to undergo transformation, the essence of human expression through music will never change. The future is revealing a seemingly incredible world of computer-based wizardry, yet the technology itself is neutral and is capable of reflecting the human spirit only insofar as the creation of music is a mirror of that spirit.

# Bibliography

Apel, Willi, editor. *The Harvard Dictionary of Music.* Cambridge, Massachusetts: Harvard University Press, 1972.

Apel, Willi and Ralph T. Daniel, editors. *The Harvard Brief Dictionary of Music.* New York: Washington Square Press, 1968.

Carr, Ian, Digby Fairweather, and Brian Priestley. *Jazz: The Essential Companion.* London: Grafton Books, 1987.

Cooper, Grosvenor and Leonard B. Meyer. *The Rhythmic Structure of Music.* Chicago: University of Chicago Press, 1960.

Crigger, David. *How to Make Your Drum Machine Sound Like a Drummer.* Newbury Park, California: Alexander Publishing, 1987.

Feather, Leonard. *The Encyclopedia of Jazz. Second edition.* New York: Bonanza Books, 1960.

Gabriel, Clive and Rosamund Shuter-Dyson. *The Psychology of Musical Ability.* New York: Methuen and Company 1982.

Harrison, F L. and J. A. Westrup. *The New College Encyclopedia of Music.* New York: W. W. Norton and Company 1981.

Jones, LeRoi. *Blues People.* New York: William Morrow and Company 1963.

Landeck, Beatrice. *Echoes of Africa in Folk Songs of the Americas.* New York: David McKay and Company

Mills, Elizabeth and Sister Therese Murphy, editors. *The Suzuki Concept: An Introduction to a Successful Music Education: Method for Early Music Edzucation.* Berkeley California: Diablo Press, 1973.

Nketia, J. H. Kwabena. *The Music of Africa.* New York:
W. W. Norton and Company, 1974.

Pareles, Jon and Patty Romanowski, editors. *The Rolling Stone
Encyclopedia of Rock and Roll.* New York: Summit Books, 1983.

Rae, John. *Latin Guide for Drummers.* Los Angeles:
Try Publishing Company, 1969.

Schuller, Gunther. *Early Jazz: Its Roots and Musical Development.*
New York: Oxford University Press, 1986.

Stewart, Michael. "The Feel Factor." *Electronic Musician,*
October, 1987.

Whitcomb, Ian. *After the Ball: Pop Music from Rag to Rock.*
New York: Simon and Schuster, 1973.